PUBLICATIONS OF
THE INSTITUTE OF HIGHER EDUCATION

A NEW TRIMESTER THREE-YEAR PROGRAM
Thad L. Hungate and *Earl J. McGrath*

ARE SCHOOL TEACHERS ILLIBERALLY EDUCATED?
Earl J. McGrath and *Charles H. Russell*

ARE LIBERAL ARTS COLLEGES BECOMING PROFESSIONAL SCHOOLS?
Earl J. McGrath and *Charles H. Russell*

THE LIBERAL ARTS AS VIEWED BY FACULTY MEMBERS
IN PROFESSIONAL SCHOOLS
Paul L. Dressel, Lewis B. Mayhew, and *Earl J. McGrath*

ATTITUDES OF LIBERAL ARTS FACULTY MEMBERS TOWARD
LIBERAL AND PROFESSIONAL EDUCATION
Paul L. Dressel and *Margaret F. Lorimer*

THE EVOLVING LIBERAL ARTS CURRICULUM:
A HISTORICAL REVIEW OF BASIC THEMES
Willis Rudy

THE GRADUATE SCHOOL AND THE DECLINE OF LIBERAL EDUCATION
Earl J. McGrath

THE QUANTITY AND QUALITY OF COLLEGE TEACHERS
Earl J. McGrath

MEMO TO A COLLEGE FACULTY MEMBER
Earl J. McGrath

LIBERAL EDUCATION IN THE PROFESSIONS
Earl J. McGrath

LIBERAL EDUCATION AND NURSING
Charles H. Russell

LIBERAL EDUCATION AND JOURNALISM
Paul L. Dressel

LIBERAL EDUCATION AND ENGINEERING
Edwin J. Holstein and *Earl J. McGrath*

LIBERAL EDUCATION AND PHARMACY
James Newcomer, Kevin P. Bunnell, and *Earl J. McGrath*

LIBERAL EDUCATION AND MUSIC
Willis J. Wager and *Earl J. McGrath*

LIBERAL EDUCATION AND BUSINESS
William M. Kephart, James E. McNulty, and *Earl J. McGrath*

LIBERAL EDUCATION AND HOME ECONOMICS
Jeanette A. Lee and *Paul L. Dressel*

THE ACADEMIC DEANSHIP
John Wesley Gould

COOPERATIVE LONG-RANGE PLANNING IN LIBERAL ARTS COLLEGES
Earl J. McGrath

THE PREDOMINANTLY NEGRO COLLEGES AND UNIVERSITIES IN TRANSITION
Earl J. McGrath

LIBERAL EDUCATON IN THE SERVICE ACADEMIES
William E. Simons

LIBERAL EDUCATION AND SOCIAL WORK
Gordon J. Aldridge and *Earl J. McGrath*

SELECTED ISSUES IN HIGHER EDUCATION:
AN ANNOTATED BIBLIOGRAPHY
L. Richard Meeth

THE LIBERAL ARTS COLLEGE AND THE EMERGENT CASTE SYSTEM
Earl J. McGrath

THE LIBERAL ARTS COLLEGE'S RESPONSIBILITY FOR THE INDIVIDUAL STUDENT
Earl J. McGrath

Copies of these reports may be purchased from
Teachers College Press, Teachers College, Columbia University

THE LIBERAL ARTS COLLEGE'S
RESPONSIBILITY FOR
THE INDIVIDUAL STUDENT

EDITED BY

EARL J. McGRATH

DIRECTOR, INSTITUTE OF HIGHER EDUCATION
TEACHERS COLLEGE, COLUMBIA UNIVERSITY

PUBLISHED FOR THE
INSTITUTE OF HIGHER EDUCATION

BY

TEACHERS COLLEGE PRESS
TEACHERS COLLEGE, COLUMBIA UNIVERSITY

FOREWORD

In the fall of 1963 the institute of higher education of Teachers College, Columbia University, inaugurated a series of annual conferences for presidents of independent liberal arts colleges. The purpose of these meetings is twofold. First, they provide an opportunity for twenty-five chief executive officers in the colleges to hear students of higher education discuss current problems. Second, for some months before each meeting members of the Institute staff, collaborating with the institutions represented, conduct a research on some aspect of their internal operations. Comparisons among the cooperating colleges provide certain basic data which all can use in evaluating their own relative status and practices.

The subject of the first meeting was long-range planning with particular attention to curricular offerings and teaching loads. In 1964 the second conference considered problems related to the planning, building, and maintenance of the physical plant. Because of the disturbances on university campuses in 1965 the college student occupied the attention of the entire world of higher education as well as of the public generally. Since such an abundance of discussion had taken place on the subject of Berkeley and other related flurries, the Conference in 1965 made no effort to review these events or to explain them. Instead the distinguished speakers, all of whom had followed the agitations of the previous twelve months, focused their presentations on the more constructive topic of the changes in policy and practice which colleges needed to inaugurate to provide more demanding experiences for their students. Most of the speakers on that occasion gave a broader than usual connotation to the term "education." Although not overlooking

v

or depreciating the responsibility of the colleges for cognitive learning, for mastering a given body of facts, and for acquiring the skills of intellectual workmanship, the discussion leaders turned their thoughts to the broader responsibilities of institutions of higher education for the cultivation of traits of personality and character which extend beyond the realm of mere knowledge. Hence, several of the sessions were concerned with admissions standards, the counseling programs, medical and health services, and the impact of the extraclass program on student development.

Naturally the speakers were given freedom in the treatment and development of their subjects. In spite of this opportunity to handle a particular aspect of the life of the college student in any manner they wished, the papers prepared by the discussion leaders showed a remarkable lack of duplication and yet a notable thread of consistency. This volume, which combines a series of essays on student behavior and a report on research concerned with dropouts in these colleges, constitutes a valuable source of information and suggestions for action for administrative officers concerned with student activism. These treatises contain facts about and proposals for handling problems of sexual relationships, drinking, drug consumption, organized sit-ins and other forms of demonstrations, mental disturbances, and a host of other problems which college and university officers now face. Although these meetings focused primarily on the small liberal arts college much that was said applies with equal relevance and force to other types of institutions of higher education.

The officers and staff of the Institute of Higher Education wish to express their thanks to the college presidents who attended the 1965 Conference, especially to those who have been present at all three meetings beginning in 1963. Dr. L. Richard Meeth, until August 1965 a member of the staff of the Institute of Higher Education, and now Assistant to the President of Baldwin-Wallace College, one of the cooperating institutions, gave considerable assistance in organizing the program. The Director is deeply appreciative of these services. He is also indebted to Mr. William O'Connell, Jr., for assuming major responsibility for the administrative arrangements while the Conference was in session. All those who attended wish to express their gratitude to President John Fischer of Teachers College for providing the revolving fund for ad interim financing of these meetings. The Director also wishes to thank the planning committee of presidents who, at the conclusion of the meeting in December 1965, remained to assist the staff of the Institute in selecting a topic, organizing a program, and preparing a list of possible speakers for the fourth conference to be held on December 4, 5, and 6 in 1966. The topic of that meeting will be "The Roles of the

Board of Trustees, the Administration, Faculty Members, and Students in the Determination of the Purposes and Policies of Academic Institutions."

The institutions represented at the 1965 Conference were: Albright College, Allegheny College, Alma College, Baldwin-Wallace College, Beaver College, Bloomfield College, Central College, Cornell College, Elmira College, Geneva College, Hamline University, Heidelberg College, Hendrix College, Illinois College, Illinois Wesleyan University, Knoxville College, Lake Forest College, MacMurray College, Manchester College, Otterbein College, Shaw University, Simpson College, and Susquehanna University.

EARL J. McGRATH
Director
Institute of Higher Education

CONTENTS

THE LIBERAL ARTS COLLEGE'S
RESPONSIBILITY FOR
THE INDIVIDUAL STUDENT

Dana L. Farnsworth, M.D.

THE LIBERAL ARTS COLLEGE'S RESPONSIBILITY FOR THE EMOTIONAL STABILITY OF STUDENTS

BEFORE I DISCUSS THE MAIN POINTS WHICH I CAME HERE TO CONSIDER with you, I want to make two explanations. I have not always been at Harvard University. This is only an indirect way of saying that my comments are based on an experience of attending a normal school of about three hundred students (which has long since become a college), a state university with about three thousand students, attendance at a small medical school for two years followed by the final two years in one of the largest, seven years on the faculty at Williams College, eight years at Massachusetts Institute of Technology (including a year as Acting Dean of Students), and now nearly twelve years at Harvard University. Between college and medical school I spent two years in a high school, teaching chemistry, physics, general science, biology, geometry, acting as scoutmaster of a local troop and treasurer of the athletic association, together with various other chores that are often assigned to high school teachers. It is from the viewpoint of my total educational experience that I speak rather than from that of a health director alone.

The second point I wish to make is that a major weakness of American higher education, long known to those engaged in counseling, is now becoming widely apparent—namely, the (usually unconscious) failure of many faculty members to view their students as human beings with feelings and desires, that is, a failure to see them as more than mere receptacles for learning. To state the issue more diplomatically and less unfairly, faculty members of all kinds now have a great opportunity (even an obligation) to become involved in the education of their students in a more personal way than has hitherto been their general

1

custom. Impersonal education will not satisfy students much longer, especially as various pressures toward impersonality in all other phases of life become more evident.

Regrettable as the Berkeley demonstrations of 1964 were from most viewpoints, they did have one significant and important effect: They have caused a nationwide series of examinations of the relations between students and faculty (including administration) and of the influence of the quality of those relations on attitudes toward learning. The focus of interest has shifted from a single-minded preoccupation with what students do to an equal concern with what they think and how they feel about what goes on in college.

(I got that phrase from a seventeen-year-old girl who had been referred to a psychiatrist after a series of school and personal problems culminated in her running away from home. When asked, "How do you like your psychiatrist?" she replied, "He's wonderful. He's interested in me. He's interested in what I think and how I feel. My parents are interested only in what I do." She perceived a subtle point and expressed it clearly; I believe it is relevant to the subject I wish to discuss.)

This widening of interest and focus—the need for which was symbolized by the demonstrations at Berkeley and elsewhere—has developed concomitantly with growth of interest in the emotional health of college students. Since 1910, with Dr. Stewart Paton at Princeton, but particularly since World War II, psychiatric services have been increasingly common parts of college health departments. That sounds like a sweeping statement; actually it means that of the 2,300 or so institutions of learning, probably about 150 now have psychiatric services of varying sizes, and another 350 have the telephone number of some psychiatrist who may be consulted from time to time. The other 1,700 or 1,800 have to do what everybody does—the best they can considering the circumstances. Those institutions with large psychiatric departments have consistently found that many students are grossly handicapped by emotional conflicts having their origins in experiences antedating their arrival at college, yet affected for better or worse by conditions encountered in college. There is good reason to believe that of the 60 per cent of students who drop out of college before graduation, a large percentage, possibly one-half, do so because of emotional difficulties. In those colleges with selective admissions policies and adequate scholarship funds the proportion is undoubtedly still higher.

I believe the data that John Summerskill summarizes in his chapter on drop-outs in the book, *The American College,*[1] is still accurate. He summarizes the research results of the last thirty years, namely that 60

[1] Nevitt Sanford, ed., *The American College* (New York: John Wiley & Sons, Inc., 1962).

per cent of all students who enter institutions of higher education drop out and then 20 per cent of them go back to that institution or to another and eventually graduate. Thus the net drop-out rate is about 40 per cent. I can find no evidence that that is not still a reliable figure. Contrary to the opinions of many people who read *The New Yorker* in December 1962, Harvard did not invent the drop-out system, nor has our drop-out rate increased or decreased in recent years. In my opinion about half of those who drop out do so for emotional reasons. Of the 25 per cent of Harvard students who drop out (and the same can be said for Princeton and Yale), 13 per cent come back and graduate within the four years at their own institutions. We do not have any data about what happens to the other 12 per cent. Actually at Princeton a drop-out who returns has a better chance of graduating than he had when he first came; this is one of the quirks of statistics.

Behind the current interest in how students feel and think about their college experience, as well as the recent interest of psychiatrists in the emotional illnesses of students, is a tradition of interest in the personal growth of students as represented by counseling programs directed for the most part by psychologists. Leaders in this field have been Edward Williamson of Minnesota, Milton Hahn at the University of California at Los Angeles, and Donald Super at Teachers College, Columbia (especially in the area of career choice). Williamson's work typifies this approach and is well outlined in his two summary volumes on general student personnel services and vocational counseling.[2] This group is very much larger than the psychiatric group. It is much more organized and has more influence.

Most of the emotional conflicts that handicap college students have had their origin in earlier life. It is well recognized by all college psychiatrists and other counselors that parental discord is one of the most potent inhibitors of effective work and of the development of well-integrated personalities in the children who are influenced by it. If parents fail to perceive their children as separate individuals, but instead look upon them as extensions of themselves, the children often feel dominated and subsequently become hostile to their parents. Marked contrasts in values honored in the home environment from which they have come and those upheld in college, particularly those which concern religion, politics, and unfair discrimination, often produce severe stress in students. If the parents or other significant older persons in a child's life do not value or respect intellectual pursuits, he will have little incentive to do so. In talking to groups of parents I sometimes

[2] Edmund G. Williamson, *Student Personnel Services in Colleges and Universities* (New York: McGraw-Hill Book Company, 1961); and *Vocational Counseling* (New York: McGraw-Hill Book Company, 1965).

say that if you take just one variable—whether there are books in the home—the children from homes with books will do better in college. If the parents actually read them, the children will do still better, and if they show enthusiasm for them and discuss them, the children will do better yet. The parents get the point when it is made this way.

Inadequate or improper sexual education is a source of distress to many students. A pamphlet, *Sex and the College Student,* has recently been published by the Group for the Advancement of Psychiatry (GAP). A book written by a committee usually reads just that way, but this one doesn't. The committee that worked on this for nearly four years was made up of psychiatrists from Berkeley, Harvard, Yale, MIT, Roosevelt, and Wellesley, psychologists from Stanford, and a variety of consultants. In 112 pages there is no passing judgment, no moralizing, but it is crystal clear to anybody who reads the pamphlet that this subject must be treated with more respect than it has been thus far accorded. I think it will be good for the students, faculty members, parents, and anyone who is interested in a dynamically oriented discussion to read. The pamphlet is psychoanalytically oriented but its position is not extreme.

Some of our brightest students have never had to work up to capacity in high school and, having acquired poor study habits, are unable to adjust to the demands of a college of high standing. Many students come to college with little sense of meaning or purpose in their lives, being propelled there by parental and social influences rather than by well-thought-out personal reasons; many of our students are in college for excellent reasons, but not their own.

A child coming from a home with extreme permissiveness or from one with rigid and inconsistent discipline may react unfavorably to the shaping influences in the college environment.

A college, though not responsible for students' already existing emotional problems, can make them worse. It can also help its students learn how to cope with stress more effectively. Whether a student becomes more or less vulnerable to stress depends in large measure on the composite of all the influences to which he is exposed during his four years in college. For those students who have been fortunate in having been brought up in families in which the parents were good role models, worthy of emulation, who worked out their differences with love and respect for one another and for their children, and exerted firm, friendly, and consistent discipline at all times, the good college has only to reinforce the favorable traits and attitudes already well developed. For those young adults whose parents (whether separated or not) have been at odds with one another, or who have grown up under otherwise unfavorable circumstances, the college may represent a final opportunity to develop higher standards, to feel a part of an institution that has meaning for them, and to learn how to solve emotional conflicts in terms of growth and development rather than by the regressive route of developing neuroses and psychoses.

The college should not only have an interest in the emotional maturation of those students who have had psychological deficiencies in their earlier lives, but it should also be concerned with the development of young men and women who have an accurate understanding of the elements necessary for the development of strong personality and character structure and who can make use of this knowledge as they rear their own children. In other words, we ought to help free our students, by every device we can, to make original mistakes with their children instead of making the same old mistakes that have been passed down from generation to generation.

The college cannot remain aloof from problems of morals and values, all of which have a great deal to do with emotional maturity. Values are not attained in a vacuum. They have to be taught by emulation rather than precept. I am almost embarrassed to say these things because they are so obvious and yet so little appreciated. But this phenomenon—do what I say, not what I do—which so frequently characterizes parent-child relations, applies with equal cogency to the attitudes of all too many teachers. Fortunately what is learned about young adults with emotional problems is relevant to the planning of college programs.

In Kenneth Keniston's recent study of alienated students, called *The Uncommitted,* he comments that the twelve alienated Harvard students he studied are not typical of American youth, but that attempts to understand them should enable us to understand more clearly the problems and stresses of more typical lives, and the individual student's methods of coping with them. Although the young men and women in college who reject what they see as the dominant values, roles, and institutions of their society may present a variety of disciplinary problems, they are not delinquents, psychotics, or revolutionaries but merely deeply disaffected young men and women. Keniston's alienated students were not victims of social injustice or personal misfortune, but they were reacting to disadvantages apparent to the most talented, fortunate, and privileged.[3] Identification with the civil rights movement, with the protest against United States policy in Vietnam, with the plight of migrant workers, with Peace Corps activities, and the like, does not mean that all the students have the same feelings, but rather that they identify with people who have strong feelings for entirely different reasons. This is a point

[3] Kenneth Keniston, *The Uncommitted* (New York: Harcourt, Brace & World, Inc., 1965), pp. 13–18.

that is sometimes missed in lumping the disaffected together, a practice which, from our standpoint, is unrealistic.

Many of the most capable students in our colleges do not feel at home either in college or in the world outside. A Harvard student in a recent letter to *The Crimson* said, that in spite of the fact that extraordinary efforts are constantly being made to keep education personal, and friendly contacts between faculty and students frequent and cordial, "Harvard is a lonely, lonely place." Sometimes I say that a person has to be really agile to keep from having someone helping him at Harvard. We have so many people around trying to do just that. The students need a sense of function if they are to feel at home in the world. In their personal relations they do not know how to deal with their impulses, with the growing need to become adults, or with the need for belief or commitment to something. The work of the college has no real meaning for the alienated students and a sense of function is missing. Their rebellion against their families is very complex. The students reject their parents partly because the parents lack the answers the children are seeking, either in their own lives or in their own activities. Their parents are ambivalent, treating them sometimes as grown-ups, at other times as children. Students are disturbed about their inability to meet their parents' expectations. They pull up their roots in the family because they feel that only by such violent assertion can they find themselves. A sense of restlessness and alienation evolves.

In one of our research projects, we have just finished following five hundred students, 250 each in the classes of 1964 and 1965, through their entire four years at Harvard, and although the data are only beginning to be organized, it seems rather clear that the students who come from what we might call disturbed homes or where there has been insufficient support are much more likely to undergo what Erikson terms an identity crisis than are those who come from homes that are pretty well structured and supported. This is no surprise to anyone.

The issues about which students are most confused center around the use and abuse of drugs, sexual morality, the correction of social injustices (especially to minority groups), and finding some way to participate personally in the solution of any or all of these problems.

How can a college make its position clear about such issues as these? Obviously it cannot do so by requiring its students or faculty members to hold certain opinions or points of view. On the other hand, it can state explicitly the standards of behavior that are expected or that constitute the ideal.[4] For example, the attitude of the college administration and faculty toward the unwise use of drugs can be made

[4] John U. Monro, "Years of Freedom," *Harvard Alumni Bulletin,* 68:148 (November 1965).

clear. Similarly, standards of sexual behavior should be so stated that students know what constitutes unacceptable conduct and the GAP committee recommends that college administrators make their positions explicit.[5] This does not mean that you develop "McCarthy-like" police states or that you go around trying to enforce rules, but there should be principles for students to try to live up to. I say to the students themselves, in discussing this whole question: To have principles of conduct helps those of you who adhere to them, but it helps even more those of you who violate them because then you are in a position to learn from your mistakes. But if we give you no standards to work for, with, or against, then what can you do? I think I can generalize and say that many of our students are in revolt not against any standards we have imposed on them but because they cannot tell if we have any standards at all. When I say we, now, I am talking about the whole faculty. Faculty members frequently are just as confused as parents are, or as the students are, and sometimes are very rude in expressing their confusion.

As President Sachar at Brandeis said recently, and I am inclined to agree with him, such statements can be expressed in general terms rather than in specific detail, thus stimulating consideration instead of appealing to natural desires to find loopholes for evasion. John Monro and I have been debating for some time now in front of our two staffs whether the college should develop rules about drug ingestion (and about what's going to happen if these rules are violated) or whether the college should state a set of principles that will guide the members of the administrative board who have disciplinary problems. I think the decision is going in favor of the latter, because when rules are made they represent a target for students' projections of their dissatisfaction with other aspects of society—for example, their parents—and so we are postponing maturation instead of facilitating it.

Sentiment about social injustices can be expressed in a variety of ways, but particularly by giving support to those student activities and organizations that are designed to remedy social ills, not only in the immediate vicinity of the college but on the national and international stage as well.

I was out in California recently and we were discussing this point informally in one of the dining rooms. It developed that a few of the communities surrounding some of the smaller colleges have indicated, "We don't want the students interfering with anything in this community. Stay out of the mental hospitals, stay out of the jails, and so on. Let us run our own affairs; the student's job is to stay in the college and

---

[5] Group for the Advancement of Psychiatry, *Sex and the College Student* (Report No. 60; New York: Publications Office, Group for the Advancement of Psychiatry, November 1965).

study." You can see that California has more problems than we thought. To move back to the East Coast now, the nine hundred or one thousand of our students who do work in settlement houses, who teach in prisons, who visit mental hospitals, are not only broadening themselves but are also being educated in the complexity of social problems, and they are changed by it. Furthermore, they are instrumental, now that they are beginning to mature, in changing the professions that have to deal with those in prisons, with the mentally ill, and with those in substandard areas. Any time we get mixed up in a problem like this, not only are the students going to change but we are going to change, and the institutions are going to change—and that is what we want.

We hear complaints from time to time that the increasing academic requirements of colleges are responsible for the growing numbers of students who develop emotional or mental illness. Such assertions are simply wrong. In my experience, hard work does not produce mental illness among students. There is also no clear evidence that the incidence of emotional distress is greater now than in the last few decades. But we are becoming more aware of the devastating effects of emotional conflict, are now more willing to think in psychological terms, and there are more students—hence more to become ill. Most significant of all, we are discovering that many illnesses can be prevented and the loss of gifted students, which we cannot afford, can be averted. As previously stated, it is also becoming apparent that measures taken to prevent the loss of those students who may be vulnerable to emotional stress also improve the quality of the educative process for all students. Some of the desirable conditions to encourage in any college which wishes its students to become adept in handling emotional conflicts while they are at the same time acquiring intellectual power are:

1. *"Repeated challenges to the student's ability, each of which can be mastered after sustained effort."*[6] I think that comes right out of Nevitt Sanford and many people before him. The important thing is that unless we challenge our students to the limit of their ability and then aid them in mastering their tasks they are not going to progress as fast as they should. I sometimes think the custom of coming to Harvard College and then going to one of its graduate schools and then taking some postdoctoral work in the vicinity is the wrong way to go about it. It is better for students to move from one institution to another every three or four years. I remember one youngster who came to Harvard from a small church-related college in eastern Pennsylvania about five or six

[6] The phrases quoted in items 1 through 6 are from D. L. Farnsworth, *Psychiatry, Education, and the Young Adult* (Springfield, Illinois: Charles C Thomas, Publisher, 1966).

years ago. He related this episode, incidentally, at one of the Danforth conferences. He was having an awful time—Harvard was a terribly big place. He went to see Peter Elder, Dean of the Graduate School of Arts and Sciences, just before Thanksgiving and said, "Dean Elder, how many courses do you have to flunk to be dropped from the graduate school?" Dean Elder said, "Five." The student said, "I'm only going to take four," to which the Dean replied, "I know it." This was excellent psychotherapy because it said to him, "Although you are being challenged, you can make it; there's time enough; don't get worried too soon."

2. *"Maintenance of high standards of academic performance and personal behavior but with flexibility as to how these standards may be attained."* I wish that we could have more people who think of the development of integrity and the development of honesty, which of course includes integrity, and responsibility, as things which have to be achieved through trial and error, rather than take such a dim view of the individuals who violate an ethical code and overpenalize them. If our disciplinary arm tried to penalize an erring student just enough to help him learn from the experience, but not enough for him to project his hostility back to the college and blame the college for it in the first place, I think we would be doing a service. The second time is another matter; one can become a little more punitive. We should not even allow the third time to occur, except in very unusual circumstances.

3. *"Assurance that when significant changes in thinking and behavior are required of students sufficient time is allowed for suitable adaptation, if possible under conditions which add to, not decrease, their self-confidence."* Lloyd Elam, the Professor of Psychiatry at Meharry Medical College, tells me he believes they could develop more physicians in his medical school if they did not have to observe the four-year lockstep; many medical students have cultural deprivations which must be overcome as they advance through medical school. If there were a way of supporting the students for five, six, or even seven years, and continuing to improve their general education as they go along, we could get more Negro physicians, whom we desperately need, the American Medical Association to the contrary notwithstanding. But all too often, especially in the medical profession, and perhaps in others too, we tend to think it is either all or none. Some time ago, Peter Elder, at Harvard, was trying to have a rule adopted that all graduate students must get their degrees in four years as the upper limit. But the argument fell flat in faculty meeting when somebody pointed out that one of the strongest proponents of this cut-off point had taken nine years to get his Ph.D. and that he was one of our most distinguished scholars and it didn't seem quite right to eliminate such people. At any rate the limit has not been put on.

4. *"Avoidance of breaks in continuity of behavior that are too abrupt for the student to master unaided and provision for or protracted help in making such an adaptation once the excessive contrast is recog-*

nized." Thinking in geographical terms, we know that certain people, let us say those who come from one of the states of the Deep South and are pretty well indoctrinated with some of that area's ideas, must be treated with more care and more patience than somebody who is already acclimated to the more liberal standards of the east and west coasts and sections of the midwest.

5. *"Developing among faculty members understanding attitudes toward and reliable information about their students together with the opportunity for frequent constructive dialogues between students and faculty members on subjects of mutual interest."* This is right at the heart of what I am trying to get at. You might think that we who are psychiatrists mean that all faculty members should become therapists. Not at all. We merely would like faculty members to think in terms of how their students respond to their teaching as much as they think in terms of how to transmit the subject matter. That is, to put it even more simply, they should be specialists in students as well as in the subject matter.

In one midwestern university, a counselor called a given professor and said that a certain student was somewhat distressed and asked the professor to keep an eye on him because any way of helping him would be appreciated. The professor replied, "I'm paid to teach, not to be a nursemaid," and hung up the receiver—just like that! Since I do not know the professor I can speak freely; I think such a person is not fit to be a professor. I would put it that strongly.

6. *"Efforts by college psychiatrists, psychologists, social workers, and all other counselors to encourage more of the problem-solving or emotional maturation experiences of students to take place within the educational rather than the therapeutic setting."* It is the job of all engaged in counseling to make themselves unnecessary. We do not anticipate being out of work soon, but nevertheless we must push in that direction. If those of us in psychiatry dropped all our other work and just took care of the very disturbed youngsters who are in our schools, each one of us would have three hundred disturbed persons to look after. In other words, this is the wrong way to go about it. You cannot solve this problem by having more psychiatrists. You have to solve it through a realization on the part of everyone in the educational institutions that we have to deal with factors in students' thinking and feeling and do it in nonclinical ways. If each one of us in psychiatry had his share of the disturbed people in the country, each one of us would have more than a thousand patients, and you can see how hopeless that would be. We must and are trying to develop a community psychiatry to take the place of the exclusive preoccupation with treatment of the mentally ill.

Most of our present students are affected by tensions quite different from those with which the students of the thirties and forties contended. Instead of focusing their attention on the problems of a depressed economy and waging an all-out war—issues of prime concern two and three decades ago—our young people must now deal with the age-old question of how to change human nature for the better. Walter Lippmann put it this way, speaking before the Vietnam situation became a crisis: "As our relations with Russia become less tense, this will be a safer world but a much more troubled and disorderly one." It is certainly clear that when the great issue is survival there is not sufficient time and energy to devote to lesser concerns.

To return to our youngsters, they are beginning to realize that living conditions could be much better for most people if certain customs, practices, and attitudes were changed. Human brotherhood has been delayed by the bitter struggle between "those who have" and "those who have not"—whether it be expressed in terms of industrial development of nations, racial and religious discrimination, employer and employee relations, or population crises. Many of the obstacles impeding progress toward improved human relations lie deep in the personality and character structure of individuals, qualities notoriously resistant to change. Intense nationalism is only one of these manifestations.

In a recent television interview, Princeton Professor Eric F. Goldman asked Professor Samuel Eliot Morison what he considered the main obstacles to our development of a "Great Society." Morison said he was worried much more about the increasing tendencies toward juvenile delinquency and sexual promiscuity than about any other developments. But he believed we could overcome some of the more blatant of those tendencies. In response to Goldman's question, "To what do you attribute these tendencies?" Morison replied, "Just the general cussedness of man." Coming from Samuel Morison this was quite an interesting diagnosis. But our students hear us say many things that are inconsistent with our actions. Because we—and by "we" I mean society as a whole, of which the educational institutions are a part—have so many reservations involved in these questions, our kids are impatient. If this is the right thing to do, why do we not do it? They are hardly willing to wait for an explanation of whose toes are going to be stepped on if this move or that one is made. Revolution is more likely to occur when people have hope and know that a better life is attainable than when they are hopeless and resigned. An excellent discussion of this is found in Eric Hoffer's book, *The Ordeal of Change,* in which he comments on de Tocqueville's ideas of a century and a quarter before.[7] From this standpoint we live in a hopeful but troubled world, with more possibilities for Utopia than ever before, but also with more engines of destruction than most of us are able to compre-

[7] See discussion by Hoffer of de Tocqueville's ideas on this point. Eric Hoffer, *The Ordeal of Change* (New York: Harper & Row, Publishers, 1963), p. 84.

hend. Individuals (as well as nations) who are unable to organize their energies effectively may react intensely and sometimes destructively to their frustrations in trying to bring about desirable change.

Now I'm going to shift focus and look at some things through the students' eyes. We may summarize some of the important tensions or stresses to which all students must react around a few key situations:

1. *The dilemma of choice:* Opportunities, good or bad, are almost limitless. Making a choice rules out many other possibilities, any one of which might have been as interesting and rewarding as the one chosen. This may make a student feel trapped—the very opposite of freedom. Although anything may be possible, everything is not possible.

One Harvard student said, "Whenever I make a choice I see doors silently closing all about me." If a person changes his mind after he has had two or three years of preparation in a given field, it is a terribly expensive thing, so he may go on for another year or two trying to salvage his poor choice and then he cannot get out.

2. *The vast increase in the accumulation of knowledge:* "For in much wisdom is much vexation; and he that increaseth knowledge increaseth sorrow." Whether, as one commentator stated, the sage was in a bad mood the day he made this observation, or whether it represents a universal truth, is open to question. We sympathize with the librarians overwhelmed by problems of storing and retrieval, we threaten to abdicate using our brains and to use computers instead, but we give insufficient thought to the plight of the student approaching the mountains of knowledge which he must master or seem to master. We must learn how to help our students avoid confusing quantity with quality of thought or knowledge as I fear has been our mistake. I think we have a lot of people now who are learning gamesmanship rather than sincerity. One of our participant observers in a Harvard student study found that at one House there was a half-hour discussion of a certain book by a certain author, both of which were imaginary, but no one was willing to admit that he had not read it. This kind of pseudo-sophistication, I am sure, exists at places other than Harvard. Interdependence is largely replacing independence as a fact of life, and the success or even survival of the resultant society depends on the achievement of attitudes of deep respect for each other on the part of all people. This means much more concern for the development and transmission of values than we have hitherto shown.

3. *Recognition of vast social injustices everywhere:* This is another source of tension for students and one to which I have alluded earlier. The elimination of social injustice has become for many young people the moral equivalent of war of which William James spoke. Resistance to changes which will reduce such injustices on the part of otherwise well-intentioned people seems to them willfully selfish. The occasional overzealous and sometimes misguided attempts of young people to bring

about such changes may evoke so much resistance that the ideal becomes obscured or lost, embittering both the victims of social injustice and those who would remove it. I find it very difficult myself not to become irritated at the people who overstate their case, but if we do that then we miss the main point. We have to sort out the good from the more vehement protestors and make use of it, and ignore those parts which irritate us a great deal: the long hair, the rancid odor, the bad manners, and all the rest of it.

4. *Feelings of anonymity or helplessness:* Many forces combine to render the ordinary person ineffective and unnoticed, whereas the eccentric achieves much attention. Students do not want to be a hole in an IBM card. Mechanization of record keeping has proceeded faster than attempts to treat students as human beings who need good role models and many opportunities to test their ideas on their older colleagues.

5. *College perceived as a means of social and economic advancement:* The concept of a liberal education can easily become lost when a college education is sought solely for its ability to increase income. A girl, possibly from one of the colleges represented at this meeting, wrote to Professor Gray at Colorado College after his article on existentialism on college campuses appeared in *Harper's* last May and said that education is being crippled in so many of our liberal arts colleges because willy-nilly we are making them into preprofessional schools and hence the concept of liberal education has suffered. This was said by a college sophomore.

6. *A crisis in the meaning and purpose of life:* One college president told me privately that we have far too many moral illiterates even in our best colleges (where there should be no excuse for them). It may well be that students are rebelling not so much against the values we hold but because it is not clear to them what we do cherish.

When students arrive at college they have much unfinished business insofar as attaining maturity is concerned. Yet this is the period which society more or less arbitrarily assumes as marking the beginning of adulthood. College administrators and teachers make the same assumption, or they should make it, yet with reservations based on the knowledge that no one can make the transition from childhood to adulthood without support. During the college period most students experience their first taste of being treated as adults, albeit with some reservations at first. Sometimes these reservations are subtle, at other times they are explicit. The older students and the faculty pass on the customs which enable the college society to remain viable. Most college communities have learned how to control themselves when the influx of new students is gradual and their integration is systematized. If new members are introduced too rapidly in a particular college, and especially when most of them are unfamiliar or unsympathetic with the mores of the college, difficulties may result. For freshmen, special procedures are usually followed to aid them in adapting successfully to their new responsibilities. Whether procedures like "orientation week" are the best that can be devised is doubtful. In recent years the emphasis has been shifting rapidly from concentration on extracurricular activities to concentration on those activities encouraging enjoyment of or enthusiasm for intellectual pursuits. When I first went to Harvard I used to talk to the freshmen for a half hour during a part of their week's orientation, but I was able to find only one upperclassman who in later years remembered that I had given what I thought was a pretty good talk, and so we finally cut it out.

The Williams College *Alumni Review* reports a project in which the assumption is made that students come there to pursue their interests in educational things, so they were assigned books to read during the summer. Subsequently, the Williams *Record* carried an editorial accusing the faculty of causing the students to become interested in intellectual things. They said that things had gotten so bad that even some of the parents had read the books that were required. It was a very nice tongue-in-cheek editorial. We copied this idea at Harvard, and also found that it worked very well to get people who write exciting books to come and discuss them. This is a long way from some of the indoctrination periods that I have suffered through.

A new student has certain key tasks to perform as he progresses through college. He must learn to become free of dependence on his parents and other older people and to develop habits of independence. Appropriate modes of dealing with authority must be achieved and the balance between freedom and authority continually examined. He must learn how to live with uncertainty and ambiguity, particularly in matters involving the balance between love and hatred and the postponement of career decisions during pursuit of a liberal education. Developing mature attitudes toward sexuality is desirable, but in this his help from the college is far from effective. He needs to find personal security, to develop feelings of adequacy or competence, and to attain some measure of prestige or esteem. Finally, he should develop standards and value systems for guidance during the rest of his life.[8]

In my conversations with students and faculty members during the past year regarding the quality of their college, one idea is expressed in almost every extended discussion: that of concern about communication between students and teachers. In one college with a good reputation among its students and the people in the surrounding communities, students said repeatedly, "We are fortunate here. We can talk to our professors and they are interested in us." At other schools, usually

[8] Farnsworth, *op. cit.*

larger ones to be sure, the comments revealed lack of contact; no one seemed interested in the students as people, or there was no sense of community in their institutions. Not long ago I was told that at one large midwestern university a study was made recently in which 90 per cent of the graduates in the sample had had no significant conversation with any faculty member during the entire four years. This seems to me to be a rather dreadful situation. I have questioned quite a number of students at other colleges about this, and a lot of them say, "Well, I think that's a little extreme, I think at least a fifth of us knows one faculty member," or something of that sort. It is still discouraging.

At those colleges in which dissatisfaction seems to be exhibited in the most annoying ways, a sense of alienation is quite common in a great many students. The behavior of students who feel that they do not belong in today's world and who reject the values of those in authority seems well designed to arouse strong condemnation by those who prize order, respect for the established institutions of society, and adherence to high personal standards in grooming. Under these circumstances it is difficult for many persons to recognize the justice of some of the objections students voice because of their irritation at the methods of protest they have chosen.

When students protest about conditions in the college, the administration and faculty should restrain their irritation and be pleased that they are concerned enough to think about the conditions that favor effective education. The students with whom I have talked say, "The trouble is not student protest; the trouble is the students who don't protest; they are the ones who worry us." To turn down their requests for a hearing and to dismiss their protests serve only to convince them that whatever is wrong is someone's deliberate fault. From that point on whatever differences exist rapidly escalate into a power struggle between opposing forces rather than a combined search for solutions that will be both constructive and widely acceptable.

Students seldom form a homogeneous group with similar ideas about issues with which they are concerned. When novel ideas are presented to them, even by their own colleagues, they usually differ among themselves much as a group of faculty members might disagree. In the resultant discussions, opinions and attitudes are shaped and modified. Instead of differences degenerating into power struggles between groups, they can become powerful incentives for learning how societies govern themselves and how to maintain a reasonable balance between freedom and authority. When faculty and students can effectively communicate with one another so as to work cooperatively toward removing the obstacles impeding the college's progress, the highest type of education becomes possible.

One option is that a college can attempt to aid in resolving crippling emotional conflicts among its students by dealing mainly with those who are obviously disturbed. Through its health service it can arrange for consultations with the best professional persons available (psychiatrists, clinical psychologists, general physicians, social workers, and so on) and aid in securing indicated treatment if that is possible. This may include giving medical leaves of absence to those students whose problems are too severe to permit satisfactory academic achievement or those for whom necessary treatment is unavailable near the college. In either case the financial responsibility for psychiatric care belongs to the individual, his parents, or to community clinics, not to the college. The latter, however, may have a moral obligation to sponsor health insurance plans that will make it possible for students and their families to fulfill the financial obligations that result from securing appropriate treatment.

These are some of the arguments that college presidents have to make to their constituencies. I do not think it is fair to siphon off funds given for academic purposes for the treatment of individuals, but I think it is not only fair but the duty of the college to use its organizational mechanism in such a way as to develop appropriate insurance plans which are reflected either in a portion of the tuition or in special fees. We cannot just wash our hands and say it is not our problem. This is not the way our society is moving and it is not the way it should move. The students, their parents, and the faculty should be brought in on decisions as to how much we can afford or why we cannot afford not to have a good health plan.

The concept of mental health need not be stressed in a program designed to encourage integrity and emotional stability. The term has acquired so many extraneous and erroneous connotations that it excites ridicule and opposition almost as often as it elicits respect. Some of the organizations now have in their platforms the goal of eliminating mental health entirely—and for their members they have done rather well. After all, "mental health" is only a short phrase to connote a state in which life is clearly worth living. It refers to those qualities which enable an individual to learn from experience, acquire satisfaction from constructive achievement, use leisure time enjoyably and profitably, deal with stresses, tolerate anxiety, endure frustrations, and exhibit sincerity, compassion, and humane attitudes. That is all mental health is. A college has a high level of mental health when it is providing the best education its students are capable of achieving.

Another method of helping (and the two choices are not mutually exclusive) is by the establishment or improvement of counseling services, whether as functions of the dean of students and his assistants or as separate organizations allied to the dean's office. These have grown both in numbers and effectiveness during the last few decades. Usually these services and the psychiatric services of the health departments collaborate closely, although occasionally competition prevails, with tragic results for staff members and students alike.

Unfortunately the efforts of the counselors and the psychiatrists are both too little and too late in many instances. Students are frequently seen only after the handicaps resulting from their conflicts have become severe. Leaving college is often the only way out, and the counselor's chief hope is that he can aid the departing student in so arranging his life as to avoid an excessive feeling of failure and can thus facilitate return to college or an otherwise satisfactory form of rehabilitation.

The greatest need at present, so far as the encouragement of emotional maturation of students is concerned, is the active and informed cooperation of the faculty members who are not administrators or professional counselors. We can no longer afford to leave the development of character, integrity, emotional stability, and the sense of ongoing responsibility for the perpetuation of worthy values to deans and counselors. Students need help and support from faculty members of all levels. They should have from them a sympathetic understanding of the complexities involved in the transition from adolescence to adulthood. Many teachers have such an understanding and have given excellent support to the influences promoting emotional maturation, but we need many more. The effort should be made to aid all (or at least most) teachers to do what the best ones have been doing all along. The possible alternatives to such a development are not attractive, unless we see advantages in the further dehumanization of man in the service of a completely technological society.

The causes of emotional and mental illnesses (aside from those involving abnormal biochemical, physiological, or physical processes) are also relatively complex, affecting as they do every human emotion. Isolation, when not desired, is at the very heart of mental illness; in practically every instance, an emotionally disturbed person has had some impairment of communication and emotional exchange with the persons who are most significant to him. This impairment may come about through rejection or hostility shown by those around him, unfair discrimination based on prejudice, cultural deprivations, or broken families with resultant psychological deficiencies such as too little love and affection, improper role models, and inadequate or inconsistent discipline. Robert Coles, of the Harvard University Health Service, works extensively with children of migrant workers and those in areas being desegregated, and he reports that it is not involvement in violent episodes that does harm to the youngsters, it is the subtle insults to which they are exposed day after day, year after year. Being spit upon in a sit-in is as nothing compared to having to wonder whether it is possible to get an ice-cream cone in one place or to use the rest room in another, or all of the many hundreds of things that have to be decided each day. We have very little awareness of that.

When these conditions persist over long periods of time, the victims either acquire strength of character in overcoming them and go on to constructive careers or they may be unable to cope with such stresses and develop a wide variety of symptoms or signs of disturbed behavior. Why some people succeed and others succumb is not yet clearly understood, or at least not conclusively demonstrated. This is one of our big problems in community psychiatry, which is a massive attempt to deal with the basic causes of emotional and mental illnesses as near their points of origin as possible. So much has been said about identity that it is somewhat like the little girl who read a book on penguins her mother had given her: She considered it a good book but it had a little more about penguins than she really wanted to know. So it is with identity and still there is a lot more that could be said about it.

What can a liberal arts college do to further widespread awareness of these disintegrative forces in our society and make long-term constructive moves to weaken and eliminate them? Speaking as a psychiatrist, I want to say that we should be teaching our students not by precept but by example. I have elsewhere discussed this problem in terms of goals of education which we might consider as supplements to those traditionally held to be the responsibility of institutions of higher learning. These should supplement, not replace, the traditional goals of education. They are as follows:[9]

1.   Respect for all persons, regardless of their race, color, ethnic background, religion, or behavior at the moment. (The latter was included because of the almost conscious refusal to put to work what is known about human behavior in the field of chronology.)
2.   Sufficient knowledge of other people to be able to judge in a general way what their needs are, the ideals they honor, the customs they practice, and the frustrations they endure.
3.   Knowledge of the qualities required in a person who can be at home with diverse groups of people and yet can enjoy being alone. I think we are teaching ourselves to be busy all the time, at least emotionally. Harold Taylor said, apropos of transistor radios, that at last we will never have to walk alone.
4.   A sensitive and perceptive awareness of one's own nature, both

[9] D. L. Farnsworth, "The Search for Identity," a lecture presented in the Edoardo Weiss Lecture Series on "Stress and Adaptation: The Age of Anxiety," Des Plaines, Illinois, September 8, 1965 (to be published in 1966).

those qualities which are under the control of the will and those which are not.

5.   Sufficient modesty and humility not to feel impelled to impose one's own ideas on others.

6.   The achievement of a proper balance between self-regard and a concern for the welfare of others. If I had anything to say about the mothers of the students I look after, it is that they are self-centered. They are trying too hard; they mean well but they smother their youngsters and excite hostility when they are really trying to give love, and this because of their inability to develop the kind of social thermometer that is needed to appreciate what goes on as a result of one's own activities.

7.   The ability to appreciate how one's own self is perceived by others (that is the social thermometer idea), thereby enabling the individual to modify his own actions continually in order to increase his competence and capacity to relate to others. Recently I was at a meeting where an old-time dean of students was talking about the current student protest; he said all the right things, but in 1935 terminology and in such a way that every student in the audience was absolutely furious. This fellow is a very good friend of mine and I thought, "Why can't he get that social thermometer going?"

8.   The quality of being able to disagree with others without becoming angry, or to disagree without becoming disagreeable; a conviction that differences of opinion should be settled by the power of rational authority rather than by force, whether verbal or physical. At the same time the value, even the necessity, of righteous (or judicious) indignation should be realized.

9.   The habit of inquiry and doubt, practiced in such a way as not to produce either fanatics who see simple solutions to complex issues or cynics who see no merit in any constructive activity.

10.   The capacity to formulate the nature of problems not yet apparent and the ability to plan the development of appropriate solutions. I think it is at the heart of the educational process to keep the mind open, but yet not to preclude its being made up intermittently. It is very difficult for students to deal with ambiguity; it is difficult for us, too. I think many of the frightened people who join "hate" groups are unable to change and so have to find simple answers, whether they really exist or not.

Obviously these principles cannot be taught directly, but they should serve as starting points for discussion of the intricate processes by which young people acquire values from others. Even when they evoke opposition, as they inevitably would in many situations, the attempt to define better goals would be constructive.

Perhaps the most important contribution a college can make toward the emotional stability of its students lies in its opportunity to show how a community can govern itself with the interests of everyone being considered but without the exploitation of any individual or group.

The basic principles that should motivate such an ideal college are consistent with, and often identical to, those that are desirable in any other institution or in democratic governments as well.

In a college which attempts to be a model of a reasonable community, the academic standards should be as high as the intellectual capacities of its students permit. Individual differences would, of course, be recognized, but the basic ideal is that each student be expected to work in accordance with his ability (which a rigid grading system discourages). I am not opposed to grading systems, but to their rigid overuse. Faculty members should be as interested in the personal and intellectual development of their students as in their own skill in acquiring and imparting knowledge. As models of reasonable men to their students, they should refrain from indulging in feuds and from taking adamant positions on any topic on which honest men may disagree. The all too frequent custom of reviewing books in a manner almost insulting to the author is a practice which I think should be deplored. The tendency to judge a colleague in unnecessarily derogatory terms does not escape the students; it tends to play into the hands of those who use methods of criticizing others which are decidedly abrasive. In a college which attempts to be a reasonable community, the faculty's consistent emphasis would always be on *what* is right, rather than on *who* is right. In the maintenance of discipline an effort should be made to keep specific rules at a minimum, but principles should be explicit, with various avenues of discussion always being kept open between professors and students for exchanges of opinions and information when proper courses of action are in doubt or frank disagreement occurs. Existing regulations should be enforced fairly and flexibly, with all students being given a second chance (if their conduct was honorable) after having dropped out of college, either for reasons of their own or by request. Most important of all, the college administration and faculty should show the utmost imagination and ingenuity in making the college experience relevant to the past experiences of its students and to broad cultural, social, spiritual, and scientific issues which will confront them in later life. College is not preparation for life, but it is that significant portion of life in which fearless examination of all previous assumptions is possible and in which plans are made for new approaches to the age-old problems that are still awaiting solutions. Students must be encouraged to deal with change and uncertainty in such a way that they can, after termination of formal education, find solutions to problems which originally could not be envisaged.

In the ideal college no one person or group should be permitted to acquire excessive power. In acute crises someone must act, and usually that person will be the president. His actions, even in such times of stress, should reflect a profound knowledge of the balance of forces acting upon all the other sources of power within and without the institution. Every interested group should be heard. The trustees, faculty, alumni, parents, citizens of the surrounding communities, legislators, foundations, and private donors all have interests and desires which must be heard and respected. The idea that students should be unquestioning recipients of the college's generosity is outmoded. They should not run a college, but neither should they be ignored or treated as children. After all, they will soon become alumni, professors, trustees, parents, citizens of local communities, legislators, private donors, or even college presidents. I have told some of them that if they just kept their minds made up they would have it made, because they would soon outnumber us; the trouble is that as soon as students leave college and start raising their own families, they become conservatives. If their college experience seems to them in retrospect to be honest, exciting, satisfying, and conducive to the adoption of the highest standards of thought and action, we will have an increasing number of allies in our own aspirations. We cannot dictate the nature of their actions; but we should at least try to stimulate our students to accomplishments beyond those we have been able to achieve.

Nevitt Sanford

THE DEVELOPMENT OF SOCIAL RESPONSIBILITY THROUGH THE COLLEGE EXPERIENCE

ONE OF THE EARLIEST REVIEWS OF *The American College*[1] APPEARED IN a Polish newspaper. It approved of the general approach to the analysis of the college as a social institution but took exception to what we seemed to regard as the goal of college education, that is, individual development. The reviewer took the position that the true goal of higher education was the improvement of society, and that one could measure the success of a particular institution only in terms of the actual contribution to society which its graduates made.

What is the answer to this criticism? I think it is true that *The American College* had little to say about social responsibility, and that it regarded the fullest possible development of the individual as the central purpose of college education. Yet, I believe we assumed, as did the Declaration of Independence, that fully developed individuals would naturally be concerned for the public welfare. We may continue to hope that this is so.

I want to argue in this paper that the person who is socially responsible in the best sense of the term is one who *voluntarily* acts in the public interest, who is dependably committed to socially valuable actions because such commitment is an integral feature of his personality, and who finds personal fulfillment through carrying out responsibilities to other people. The argument, in other words, is that in a democratic society we cannot separate the needs of the individual and the needs of the society; the two must be fulfilled together.

Some of the socialist countries, such as Poland and Russia, have

[1] Nevitt Sanford, ed., *The American College* (New York: John Wiley & Sons, Inc., 1962).

shown that they know a great deal about how to win young people's devotion to the purposes of the state. These countries have the great advantage of a more or less universally accepted value-orientation; parents, schools, and government officials all say essentially the same things to young people about what they should do and be. Like other relatively underdeveloped countries, Poland and Russia also have a national concern with increasing production. This is a great benefit when it comes to helping young people to feel useful and to see their place in the society. There is nothing to suggest that these young people, at least while they are still in their teens, do not feel that they are giving freely of themselves. There is not even evidence to suggest that this kind of all-out emphasis on social responsibility when young people are in school necessarily impairs future development of the personality. University students show considerable capacity for dissent, and it seems obvious that the countries could not operate if all responsible adults could do nothing but conform automatically with dictates from above.

The fundamental question is whether the kind of social responsibility to be observed in the young can be attained without the development at the same time of an essentially ethnocentric outlook, that is to say, whether the ingroup solidarity does not depend on the existence of outgroups—bourgeoisie, aggressor nations, and so on—that can be categorically rejected and hated. If this is true, there is the further question of whether a nation that leaves the great mass of its citizens with this general outlook can be said to accomplish very much.

This is not intended to imply that the socialist nations have any monopoly on nationalistic patriotism. It can be found in some degree in every country and is something which governments generally tend to encourage. While I saw plentiful evidence of it in the Soviet Union, it is all of a piece with the patriotism we try to promote here at home with such devices as the pledge of allegiance to the flag.

The higher order of social responsibility which we seek to develop through college education consists of loyalty to certain *ideals* which the individual understands rather than to an aggregation of people whom he regards as just like himself. Naturally loyalty to these ideals may be accompanied by some opposition to other, opposing ideals, but opposition to people will be on a basis of their behavior or principles, not on the basis that they are categorically different and therefore somehow inferior. This spirit does not permit categorical rejection of entire groups of people, whether minorities within the nation or national groups outside. The expectation that all people can become like oneself —or the self one would like to be—is fundamental to the democratic ideal.

For most people, however, social responsibility involves some loyalty

24   NEVITT SANFORD

to the group itself, as well as to its ideals. Here we have to ask, "Responsibility to *what* society or to *what* social aggregate?" Loyalty to and responsibility for one's family certainly have value, but they do not represent a very high level of individual achievement; they develop more or less automatically in human societies. The same can be said for tribal loyalties. If they do not develop automatically, at least it is no great trick to produce them. The individual who finds himself caught up in such loyalty, who uses it as the primary guide for his behavior, and who has never had occasion to compare the object of his loyalty to other objects cannot be said to have developed very much.

From the point of view of general human welfare, to regard tribal or national loyalties as ultimate values would leave the world as a collection of warring camps. Peace—or even survival—demands social responsibility that is relatively free of ethnocentrism. No matter how devoted to social duties a person might be, no matter how great his willingness to sacrifice himself in the service of society, so long as he feels either the desire or the duty to exclude some people from the full benefits of that society, we cannot say that he has developed a high level of social responsibility or that he is not in need of further education.

We come now to the question of what the colleges are doing to develop this kind of mature social responsibility and how well they are succeeding. During the 1950's a good deal of criticism was heard on this point. Jacob, mainly on the basis of the Cornell Values Study, pointed out that students were concerned with only the narrowest sphere of interest; that they were focused on themselves, their families, and their futures—on how they were going to benefit from our society, but with never a mention of what they might do for it.[2] Another interesting study, by Gillespie and Allport,[3] compared the outlook of our students to that of students in a dozen other countries. For example, to an Egyptian villager an education meant the opportunity to do something for his people; to our students it meant an opportunity to spend summers on Cape Cod. Riesman[4] and Keniston[5] made observations of the same kind, the former coining the expression "privatism" to describe the orientation of American college students of the fifties.

During this period, we were studying students at Vassar College, and we did find that, compared to earlier generations, these girls were intent

---

[2] Philip E. Jacob, *Changing Values in College* (New York: Harper & Row, Publishers, 1957).

[3] James M. Gillespie and Gordon W. Allport, *Youth's Outlook on the Future* (Garden City, New York: Doubleday & Company, Inc., 1955).

[4] David Riesman, *Constraint and Variety in American Education* (Garden City, New York: Doubleday & Company, Inc., 1958).

[5] Kenneth Keniston, "Inburn: An American Ishmael," in Robert W. White, ed., *The Study of Lives* (New York: Atherton Press, 1963).

on getting married and leading comfortable lives. What impressed us more, however, was the fact that these students were nevertheless changing during college in what we considered to be favorable ways. In general, they became less ethnocentric and authoritarian, more independent in their thinking, and more critical of our social institutions, yet at the same time they became more accepting of themselves and other people. It seemed to us that such changes in a student promised well for her future even though she was not at the time expressing any great intentions to go out and reform the world.

Today, in sharp contrast to the fifties, the criticism is likely to be that students are taking *too* much interest in social affairs. There is a feeling that students are too preoccupied with public issues, social action, and other things they really know nothing about. What has made these students change?

The answer, in my view, is that students have not changed. It is the times that have changed, and college students are merely reflecting the general climate of opinion in the country at large. In writing about students during the fifties, my inclination was not to blame them for their conformity but to point instead to the state of affairs in the nation as a whole. The last decade was not a very happy time in this country; the cold war was in full swing, and the nation seemed to be caught up in a surly, automatic anticommunism. There was great pressure on students to adapt themselves to, and to take their place in, a society that was assumed to have developed as much as it needed to or was going to and only needed to be defended against its enemies. There was little to inspire sensitive or idealistic young people. If students today are different, we must credit this mainly to differences in the outlook of the whole society. Developments such as the civil rights movement, the Peace Corps, and the fresh accent on social welfare—things which have captured the imaginations of many students—could as well have inspired people who were in college in the early 1950's.

Even today, the proportion of students who are involved in social action is commonly overestimated by the man in the street. Katz, in a longitudinal study of student development at Berkeley and Stanford, concluded that only about 15 per cent of the students were at all involved in what might be called "activism"—whether in demonstrations or in field work such as tutoring students in the Negro ghettos.[6] The great rank and file of students are the same as ever—something which I do not doubt many people will find reassuring. As a matter of fact, the number of students who display any interest whatsoever in public

[6] J. Katz, "The Learning Environment: Societal Expectations and Influences," a paper presented at the 48th Annual Meeting of the American Council on Education, Washington, D.C., October 6–8, 1965.

TABLE 1.   PERCENTAGES OF STANFORD AND BERKELEY MEN AND WOMEN EN-
GAGING IN DIFFERENT ACTIVITIES WITH DIFFERENT DEGREES OF FREQUENCY*

	FREQUENTLY				OCCASIONALLY				NEVER OR ALMOST NEVER			
	Stanford		Berkeley		Stanford		Berkeley		Stanford		Berkeley	
	M	W	M	W	M	W	M	W	M	W	M	W
Civil rights activities in or near school	4	7	4	5	16	20	14	19	81	73	82	73
Civil rights activities in other states	1	1	0	0	4	3	0	1	95	94	99	97
National or community political activities	4	4	4	2	26	34	22	27	70	62	74	70
Campus political activities	8	8	7	4	23	26	21	24	69	66	78	71
Service activities off-campus, e.g., work with the unemployed, minorities, etc.	8	9	3	10	17	31	12	33	75	59	84	39
Student committees, etc.	15	22	7	14	38	42	23	29	47	34	70	57

* Approximately 500 Stanford men and women—about one-half of the graduating class—and approximately 600 Berkeley men and women—about one-third of the graduating class.

affairs is very small. At the beginning of the Student Development Study at Stanford, in 1961, the interview included an item about interest in public affairs. After about two-thirds of the freshman sample was interviewed, it was discovered that no one had indicated such an interest, and the item was dropped. A question bearing on the same topic was included on the senior questionnaire four years later, however. (The sample to which it was given was not necessarily representative; it was made up of students who had taken part in a survey of freshmen and were now easily persuaded to fill out a questionnaire. This in itself suggests that if it is biased, it is in the direction of greater social responsibility.) The question was: "Which of the following experiences or activities have you engaged in during your college years?" Then some twenty-two activities were listed and the students were asked to check the frequency of their engagement in them. The responses are shown in Table 1.

These same students were asked to list those organizations, clubs, and the like that had been most important to them during their college years. Very small proportions—never more than 10 per cent—of the Stanford and Berkeley men and women listed civil rights groups, other action groups, political groups, or political problems study groups.

The picture is much the same when students are asked how they view their future lives. The task was "Rank the following interests and activities according to the *relative* degree of importance you expect them to have in your life after graduation." Then followed a list of fourteen items including "Participation in activities directed toward national or international betterment," "Participation as a citizen in the affairs of your community," and "Helping other people." Very few students ranked any one of these three activities first, second, or third in order of importance. Eleven per cent of the Berkeley women assigned "Helping other people" a rank of 3 or higher, but no other group of students— Stanford or Berkeley men or women—gave any one of the activities so high a rank in more than 7 per cent of the cases.

The single event which most attracted public attention to student activism was, of course, the Free Speech movement at Berkeley. Yet even this involved only a relatively small minority of the total population of the university. In the fall of 1964, at the height of the controversy, Professor Somers of the Sociology Department questioned a representative sample of Berkeley students about their attitudes on the matter.[7] It was inferred that of 27,500 students, about 30 per cent agreed with both the goals and the tactics of the "militants" (as Somers called them), another 30 per cent agreed with the goals but not the tactics, and 22 per cent were against both goals and tactics. Quite a few were undecided. Even of those who were sympathetic to the cause, most usually sat on the sidelines. The largest demonstration ever staged there had six thousand participants—less than one-fourth of the student population. Those who sat-in in Sproul Hall, presumably the most dedicated, numbered only some eight hundred. Somers points out that over half of the militants were simply going along with parents who held similar views.[8] Some of the young men, for example, were the sons of faculty members at nearby institutions and their fathers were supporting their stand.

The six thousand who demonstrated for "free speech" in 1964 were not really very different, I think, from the five thousand who in 1950 signed a petition in support of the professors during the loyalty oath controversy. And the "campus radicals" of the thirties were probably almost as numerous in proportion as the "activists" of today— numerous enough so that colleges such as Vassar were seen by the citizenry as hotbeds of radicalism.

The phenomenon of politically uninterested students, most of whom

[7] R. H. Somers, "The Mainsprings of Rebellion: A Survey of Berkeley Students in November, 1964," in S. S. Wolin and S. M. Lipset, eds., *The Berkeley Student Revolt* (Garden City, New York: Doubleday & Company, Inc., 1965).
[8] *Ibid.*

are carrying on the conservative views of their parents, is not unique to this generation either. I can remember that when we were in college the efforts of professors to interest us in national affairs were really in vain. One professor in particular tried in every way he could think of to interest us in the great events of the time, but his words fell on deaf ears as far as I was concerned. The events that really concerned us were mostly on campus—on the football field and sometimes midway between our college and the women's college across the lake. We were interested in where we lived and not in the larger world, and that is true of most students. The pressing educational problem still centers on the great mass of students who are not caught up in activities, who are in a stage of development at which serious social concern is probably not even usual.

THEORY OF PERSONALITY DEVELOPMENT

If colleges hope to do more than they are now doing to develop a high level of social responsibility, they will have to be guided by theory and knowledge concerning the way in which social responsibility develops in the human personality.

I would start by saying that a child is by nature a social being, that he develops interaction with other people. He needs them and in time develops attachments to them. In order to sustain these attachments he has to carry out some obligations to the people around him, but this is not just on a *quid pro quo* basis. He is hardly to be differentiated from the social group in which he lives, and he loves others in much the same way others love him. He incorporates in his personality much of what is in the social environment. If his social environment is loving, he tends to be loving himself, so that his obligations to other people become closely tied to his obligations to himself. Gross failures in social responsibility, such as selfishness or aggressive self-seeking, are always tied to failures or distortions in these early social relationships.

A child normally desires to give something to others, to give himself to causes or to enterprises in which he can participate with others; this is an integral part of his need to be protected and loved, and the basis of his good conscience and his self-respect. Indeed the young person is normally idealistic, chiefly as an outcome of his struggle with his own antisocial impulses. In order to overcome his badness, he strives for a kind of perfection. As is natural in so undeveloped a personality, the young person who is in this stage of wanting to do good sets for himself high goals of moral achievement and at the same time has high expectations of other people. In childhood, then, the inclination to be a social being takes root. The adolescent years bring a shift in attachment from the family to a group outside the home and the development of intense group loyalty. Adolescents normally like to lose themselves in the group, to be fully accepted by it, to be fully identified with its purposes, and to be uncritically loyal to the group and indiscriminately hostile to out-groups that threaten it. At this time ideas of right and wrong tend to be based on the thinking of the group. The individual wants to perform hard tasks in the interest of the group and to be rewarded by that group for what he does.

This unquestioning loyalty and devotion are easily generalized to larger social groups such as the nation, in which event we find the kind of nationalistic patriotism discussed earlier. I would refer to this uncritical devotion to the group as a lower order of responsibility. It does not require much education or even very much intelligence. It is the kind of thing we have in athletic teams, combat groups, Komsomols, and the like. All nations make use of this kind of devotion in carrying out their purposes.

The question is, can nations do this without imposing some restrictions on the freedom of the individual. And also, can an individual who is quite free nonetheless be counted on to devote himself to group purposes as needed. The trouble with lower-order social responsibility based on narrow group loyalty is that it is likely to be rather fleeting. It dissolves when the group dissolves, and constantly needs to be sustained by group influence. Probably all conscience needs some kind of external support, but one of our aims in the development of conscience is that it sustain the individual in the absence of immediate support by the social group.

To understand group loyalty we must see it in a developmental perspective. It serves the developing individual as a means for controlling himself, for knowing what to do and what not to do, in the absence of family influence. As the individual passes into the larger society, the development of group loyalty is a first step toward being a full member of the social group. I would argue that one who can go through this stage and then grow out of it, as he necessarily becomes more critical of the group's purposes, will be less likely to fall back on blind loyalty and uncritical rejection of other groups than if he had never gone through it at all. Further, I would say that if this is a normal stage of development—and I think it is—then a youngster who does not pass through it in high school ought to have a chance to do so while he is in college. There is plenty of opportunity for this kind of group spirit in sports, in fraternity life, and in other areas; we all know students who got a lot out of this during their first two years, but tired of the "rah-rah" by the time they were juniors and seniors.

More disturbing, in my opinion, is the superintellectual youngster who has never had group experience in high school years, who was always his mother's boy, who did not play with rough fellows but came home to study. When he goes to college, he has a blanket rejection of sports, fraternities, everything that in our society is part of normal life among men. He goes on to be an intellectual who feels alienated from the rest of the world. He cannot live any place except at a college, and does not feel at home with anyone other than intellectuals.

While we ought to regard some sort of group loyalty as normal and probably desirable at certain stages, it seems clear that if social responsibility is to be dependable, it has to go beyond this. If it is to be more than just group conformity, more than a compulsive need to "do one's duty," it must somehow be connected with the persisting needs of the personality. We want a state of affairs in which a man loves his socially responsible work because he finds in it the satisfaction of a whole range of needs—both his higher needs for self-respect and his lesser needs for mastery, achievement, self-expression, or even vanity. In a fully integrated personality, socially responsible behavior can actually be a channel through which a whole range of needs can be expressed, childish needs as well as higher ones. One can, if he is sufficiently developed, find in group solidarity some of the same kind of wholeness that the child enjoys, only now it is on a totally different level. One can also be devoted to the social group because now one is able to separate the bad from the good and settle for the good even though there is a little bit of bad in the picture.

If one is going to pass from adolescent group loyalty to mature social responsibility, he has to pass through a phase in which the group's goals and purposes are examined and then accepted in some part. The truly responsible individual must be able to go along with the purposes of the group *after* he has subjected these purposes to his best judgment and intelligence. In other words, he will believe in its purposes, not because of social pressure or tradition or fear, not because other alternatives have not been considered, but because he has examined these purposes and decided that they are the best that he can find. He can also see that his own purposes can be realized through responsibility to the group.

In order to reach this stage of development the individual must be given a chance to criticize the group—the national group or the local group—and to compare it with others. He must probably pass through a phase of disenchantment with his college, his community, his nation. Students do. At this stage we see them complaining about all the hypocrisy, all the phoniness around them. They are very prone to see failings in adults and in the ways of the major society. Some apparently make a big thing of this and become alienated from society out of disappointment, out of discovering that great people have feet of clay, and so on. Some, I daresay, nonetheless eventually see that such is life, unfortunately, and that they have to accept some of the bad along with the good and carry on.

By the same token, I think a certain relativity of values is the normal state in college students. After they have been introduced to anthropology and after they have listened to a few lectures on sex, they often come to the view that we have one way of doing things and others have another, and there is little to choose between the two. Normally, students pass through this phase in which they suddenly feel that there is simply no basis for choosing among alternatives. "What is good for her," as the Vassar girls used to say, "might not be good for me." They may complain that the college has deprived them of all their value-orientation without giving them anything to take its place. We may nonetheless hope that they will find something to replace those lost values, and we can assume that, when they do, they will have given some thought to the matter and not accepted the new values automatically.

THE TASK OF THE COLLEGE

From a developmental point of view, the task of the college is a large one. Freshmen are not very far along toward development of the kind of social responsibility of which I speak. Generally they are pretty much in the ethnocentric phase of group loyalty. They are still caught up in problems of authority and inclined, when the chips are down, to do what authority says rather than what they themselves have thought about. They are in a very poor position to take responsible action on the larger social front, often because they lack self-confidence and have a very uncertain view of what they can do. They are also taken up with other problems. For the freshman, major developmental tasks still lie ahead. Soon he is so caught up in his personal problems that he is in no position to worry about other people's problems, to say nothing of the larger world, about which he typically knows very little.

There is evidence that development in the direction of mature social responsibility occurs in the liberal arts college. We have observed this directly in students at Vassar, and at Stanford and Berkeley. This evidence is not simple and direct, however. When students are asked to respond to an attitude scale made up of items that state what a good citizen ought to do, or express approval of existing institutions, seniors actually obtain *lower* scores than do freshmen. In the California Psychological Inventory[9] there is a scale labeled "Social Responsibility." In

[9] H. G. Gough, *California Psychological Inventory Manual* (Palo Alto, California: Consulting Psychologists Press, Inc., 1956).

the middle 1950's, Vassar seniors scored lower than freshmen on this instrument. We took this to mean—and other evidence has supported the view—that as they went through college, Vassar students changed in the direction of greater independence of thought, greater freedom from conventionality, greater capacity for nonconformity. In other words, they moved away from what I have called lower-order social responsibility. Knowing some of these seniors, we did not believe for a moment that their increasing skepticism or even cynicism concerning family, church, and state would lead them to neglect their civic responsibilities or to be unresponsive to human needs. What we found reassuring was the fact that these increasingly independent, critical, and nonconforming young women were the very ones who showed the sharpest decline in ethnocentrism and authoritarianism. As their faith in institutions went down, their faith in themselves and in people generally went up. We did not doubt that they would be responsive to adult leadership in actions aimed at improving the general welfare, or that when they found themselves functioning within our institutional structure they could be counted upon to take their part.

WHAT CAN THE COLLEGE DO?

The question is, what can the college do to favor the development of mature social responsibility. Some colleges do very well with some students. How can more students be reached? What kinds of educational procedures promote the development of social responsibility? I think I have said enough to suggest that social responsibility is a complex orientation made up of values and knowledge, and of relationships of this orientation to the rest of the personality. Not only must the individual value social responsibility, but his sense of social responsibility must be sustained through connection with the rest of the personality. This cannot very well be the case unless the structure of values and needs is supported by knowledge.

In our country, when we talk about developing social responsibility, it is mostly under the heading of citizenship education. We naturally think first of a curriculum—of courses in citizenship, government, international relations, political science, and the like—on the assumption that if people are going to contribute to our society they have to know how it works. Recently the effort has been made to enrich classroom work with field demonstrations or field trips to Washington to show students how the system works. I would regard this as essential but somehow minimal. We cannot expect students to become socially responsible merely through these appeals to the cognitive. As a matter of fact, students tend to regard these courses, even those that include field trips, in the same way they regard all other courses; namely, as something one takes examinations on, not something intended to touch one's life in a fundamental way. Yet the fact remains that it is precisely this knowledge that must become the basis for their criticism of the society—criticism which is absolutely essential if the student is going to outgrow lower-order social responsibility.

When we speak about changing values in college or notice instances in which values have changed, our first image is probably that of the student who becomes loyal to a new institution; namely, the college and what it stands for. If we wish to change values, we put the student in a community in which other values are represented; we make him a member of that community and expect that he will gradually assimilate its culture. Newcomb demonstrated this assimilation at Bennington College.[10] The longer the student stayed at Bennington, the more she shared the general Bennington outlook. The faculty and the older students represented a kind of consensus on values, and new students gradually came to accept this. The same point has been vividly demonstrated at St. John's College, Annapolis, where there has been one faculty-student culture. The students who stay there have virtually no alternative to participating in this culture.

I think that this is also the sort of thing that held at Vassar so strongly in the early days and gave Vassar girls the feeling that they were obligated to contribute to society. This dedication is very marked in the graduates of the early thirties whom we were able to study as alumnae. Mary McCarthy notes that some of the women in *The Group* have a nagging feeling that because they were Vassar girls, they should be doing something for society.

Now this kind of social responsibility is just a cut above the adolescent group loyalty described above. One might say that a traditional value-orientation has been exchanged for a prevailing one. Conscience has changed in its content but not necessarily in its structure, nor in its connections with the rest of the personality. We noticed that if a Vassar woman, after imbibing the Vassar culture, married a man who was somehow representative of the same outlook, they retained the social responsibility they developed in college. If, on the other hand, their marriage meant moving into a community with values quite different from those of Vassar, there was a tendency for them to lapse back to the outlook they had before they went to college.

Having a college stand for something, espousing a value-orientation which it attempts to put across to its students, is a minimum requirement if we are to develop social responsibility. The extraordinary thing is

[10] Theodore M. Newcomb, *Personality and Social Change* (New York: Dryden Press, 1943).

how often these minimum requirements are not fulfilled in colleges and universities today—perhaps particularly in the universities. Students are hard put to find in these institutions models for the social responsibility we would like to have them develop. Too rarely do they find in the leadership even the consistency and honesty that would seem to be minimal. In the universities, I think the students rarely encounter among faculty members much loyalty to the purposes of the whole institution. The faculty are mostly department men, and each department is seen as an independent principality to which loyalty is to be given. Beyond that nothing else seems to matter very much. (All other departments belong to enemy territory!)

Rarely are students told what the purpose of their education is or that one purpose might be to enable them to contribute to society. Usually the message that they get is, "You had better look after yourself." Most of the promised rewards are in terms of self-satisfaction through success in one's vocation or profession. Most of the appeals are to self-interest and most of the demands are made in those terms. Nor are students often told that they must do something because they are going to be leaders of society and that it expects some great things of them.

Students have little chance even to feel that they are capable of giving anything to anybody else. In today's high-pressure system, their problem is to survive; and if one is barely surviving, he will naturally have some difficulty in thinking of himself as a person who can lead others and give to others. Being in college, for most students, is being in slavery of a sort. It is quite a jump from that to leadership in socially responsible ways. Perhaps in the situation of today, when the colleges and universities have so many things to do, it may be enough to ask that they conduct themselves so that not too many students lose the idealism with which they began.

To integrate social responsibility with the rest of the personality is the aim, and it is mainly through intellectual work of the right sort that this is to be accomplished. We cannot expect students always to maintain a value-orientation acquired merely through conformity with the ways of a college community. Nevertheless we should not regard such an acquisition lightly. It is likely to be superior to the outlook with which the student arrived at college, it *may* be maintained if the student moves on to a community that provides enough support, and it favors the development of an internalized disposition to social responsibility.

Our goal is to expand both the area of the intellect and the area of motive and feeling, and then to bring the two together in a larger whole. To this end we try to mobilize the student's deeper needs and emotions in the interest of intellectual strivings and, at the same time, we try to bring intellect to bear on the things he cares most about. If he has a good intellectual grasp of important matters then we may anticipate his taking action with respect to them, but this is not likely to happen unless his feelings are aroused; if he has appropriate feelings about things, the right instincts as we say, and is inclined to action, then we want to make sure that he knows what he is doing. As suggested above, the great majority of students need to be waked up, to have their feelings aroused in connection with the great social and political issues of the day. But these concerns must be put in an intellectual context if the student is to get beyond mere feeling or mere conformity with group pressures. We want his social concerns not only to be based in deep feelings but to be a part of his most conscious self; for this to come about, these concerns must become the object of the student's own thought and judgment and decision making.

In our educational endeavors, then, we should be passionate about intellectual matters, and intellectual about matters that have aroused passions. The most controversial issues of the day are precisely those that should be discussed on the campus. By the same token, crises and conflicts of campus life, for example, a student-administration struggle about rules or a faculty-trustees struggle about academic freedom, should be seen as special cases of larger issues and be made subjects of intellectual analysis. Let students—and let us, too—learn to use their heads when feeling is running high, and let them learn that issues about which feelings run high are often most worthy of intellectual effort.

Now I think again of the professor who tried to interest us in the issues of the 1920's. We had one of those courses in which we read contemporary Supreme Court decisions which we were then supposed to discuss in class. I must say that my friends and I did not have time to read many of the cases and we sometimes used that class to prepare for the next one, but somehow or other there came through to us our teacher's sense of the importance of these things. Somehow his very impatience with us conveyed the idea that we should be interested in these things. Something else impressed us, too, and that was that he never gave up on us. He assumed that sooner or later we would have to be interested in these great issues, and the end of the semester found him trying just as hard as he did at the beginning. He assumed that although we were not very much, we were nonetheless the best hope of the nation, and that sooner or later we were bound to see what he was trying to put across.

Nowadays, of course, we dismiss from college young people who will not prepare their cases. In my day we did not have to worry about that possibility, for we had been given to understand that we were being depended on to take up the tasks of our society. As a matter of fact, as soon as I was through with matters that were really pressing in college, I began to read material of the sort our teacher offered, and I found it very interesting. What occurs to me now is that he should have had a way of giving us some concrete imagery of what his material really referred to. We did not have a clue, for example, as to what he was talking about when he dwelt on labor relations, because we had no imagery of either labor or their relations. I think if we were taken into the field and shown directly something of what was really involved, our teacher might have been able to connect his interest with some of our experiences and to put something across to us. I think this is better understood by educators today.

The development of full social responsibility requires the experience of participation in social actions or actions that are helpful to other people. The young person needs this experience in order to test the adequacy of his judgment, to familiarize himself with what he can and cannot do; above all, to know in a new way the self-fulfillment that comes from being of service to others.

Many college students suffer from a lack of opportunities to be of service. Their developing critical sense causes them to see many possible actions as unworthy of them; they are under great pressure not to appear soft, or unsophisticated; and the major demand on them is that they compete successfully with others and find ways to "beat the system." They pass up chances to be helpful, and thus generate a good measure of self-contempt. As this feeling toward the self builds up there is a longing for an opportunity to sacrifice oneself in some action of great significance. Nothing of sufficient significance presents itself as feasible—hence more dissatisfaction with oneself. (That this mechanism is a common one is shown by the fact that when there is a natural catastrophe, such as the New York "black-out," when there is no one to blame, most people delight in the chance to be helpful to one another.) College students whom we think of as "uncommitted" or "alienated" often seem to be in this situation. They can even make a correct intellectual analysis of themselves and their trouble without its doing any good. Probably the only cure is an actual experience of being helpful, which often can be had in some radically different setting. This experience should, of course, sooner or later be connected with or become a part of the student's intellectual activities.

I do not want to suggest that the only way to educate people to social responsibility is to involve them in social action right now. We know too little about the relationships between the patterns of college behavior and future performances in the world. Vassar women who became leaders in the community were not, in general, campus leaders nor were they as students particularly active on the social front. We know also that the British Labour Party recruited its leaders from Oxford and Cambridge students who had been studying the classics through four years of college and never gave any attention to what was going on in the contemporary world.

Too early a commitment to some pattern of social action can easily interfere with education. A premature commitment will prevent the individual from examining things in a way that he must in order to become mature. It may very well be that students who are suppressed the most in college are those most likely to become radicals later on; they may persistently strive for the freedom that was denied them earlier. Much needs to be learned before we can speak with great assurance about the connections between college experiences and later social responsibility.

Nevertheless, it seems to me that we will do best at the present time to follow the guidelines that have been sketched out above. This means that we should try again to state the social purposes for which we want students to take responsibility. This is where the contemporary student "activists" come in. I think they have made a real contribution in drawing attention to the neglect on the part of educators to state clearly enough the great purposes that our colleges are designed to serve.

It is not easy to make these statements in ways that do not sound phony to today's students. That was one of the complaints of the Berkeley student activists. The addresses on Charter Day did not sound honest because it was too easy to see discrepancies between what was said and what was done. It *is* possible to make statements about our great purposes that will get across to students, and it *is* possible to demonstrate by our own behavior that we take these purposes seriously and expect students to do so, too.

C. Robert Pace

NEW CONCEPTS IN INSTITUTIONAL GOALS FOR STUDENTS

THE TITLE OF THIS PAPER IS ITSELF, IF NOT A NEW CONCEPT, AT LEAST one which merits new emphasis in higher education today, for too often we write and talk about institutional goals for institutions rather than about institutional goals for students. The familiar trio of purposes—teaching, research, and public service—refer to activities of faculty members and administrators. If we wanted to refer more explicitly to students we would probably use such words as learning, discovery, and social responsibility. In any event, the current national discourse about higher education involves both the student and the institution, and it is in the relationship between them that abstract goals are exemplified in policies, programs, and activities.

In the recent literature of student protest the themes of impersonality, individuality, commitment, and participation are recurrent ones:

> After more than two years in a fraternity, trying to sit through courses and discover some meaning, I hit on the Tutorial Project. I dropped out of school for a year to work on it and now I recognize many changes in myself. For the first time, I'm getting good grades. I'm interested in my work and in other people. In a sense, I found my own compartment in a group with which I could identify, learn from, and then broaden out.

> You're standing there, and people just walk by, and when you try to get them to join the project, almost everyone says, "I don't have the time." Not even two hours a week. I think that is ridiculous. They want to be involved, but I think they are in some way afraid to be.

A student primarily interested in academics who spends all his time studying is making legitimate use of the University. If he's concerned with political or social action, he is using his education at the University to further his understanding of society—I think that's also good. But some people are here with no definite goal in mind, who are not to any extent guided by the University.

In one of my business classes the professor talked about Vietnam with the group, since they were all caught up on their work. The odd thing was that although normally about 15 students attended in a class of 80—since textbooks gave all the information—the classroom was filled all three days. They really wanted to know what was happening.

The University isn't democratic enough. It assumes students are adolescent in the sense that they're not going to be given any real responsibility for shaping their own environment. Students should have a share in decisions about the building program, student conduct, dormitory regulations, academic program, the curriculum, and teaching.

Many of those who went to Georgia to help Negro voters register have never been active on campus before in anything.

Sometimes I get the feeling that I'm like a particle of sand in an hour glass, going through a sort of endurance test until I receive my degree.

I had a course with more than 500 students. As the noon bells rang, and we walked out into the quad, 5000 students hurried by and I didn't see one familiar face. You feel you're all alone with thousands of people around you.

A lot of students coming here would like to get involved in something, but they simply have no direction at all. However, as they gain more confidence they begin to take advantage of the University's opportunities.[1]

In the complaints of students and the concern of professors and administrators, impersonality is usually associated with bigness and bureaucracy: large classes, long lines, hotel-like dormitories, official channels for communication, machine-graded tests, the lonely crowd, and always those IBM cards—the popular scapegoat of salvation by the numbers. However fortunately free the liberal arts colleges may be from these problems of impersonality that beset the multiversity, there is another kind of impersonality imbedded in the fabric of higher education, affecting small colleges and large universities with almost equal pervasiveness. Although the word "impersonality" is rarely used to describe it, the term fits it tolerably well. It is the impersonality of the curriculum. The subject matter is all chopped up into abstractions of reality, and

[1] Quotes from *UCLA Alumni Magazine,* 40:1 (Fall 1965).

many courses are exercises in the acquisition of a technical vocabulary, which itself is totally abstract. As a result, such courses can be passed only by students who display some substantial talent for abstract verbal learning and memory. Most courses in abnormal psychology, for example, are not about abnormal people but about abstracted phenomena such as neurosis, psychosis, regression, sublimation, projection, transfer, anxiety, and the like. It is quite possible for a student to be getting an *A* in abnormal psychology while being totally unaware that his roommate is having a breakdown. And consider, for example, the vocabulary component of a basic college course in geology, or physical anthropology, chemistry, genetics, economics. Even in art or music many courses are courses in the acquisition of a specialized analytical or descriptive vocabulary and rarely involve the student in any direct experience with the creative process and its personal meaning.

Along with this emphasis on vocabulary and abstractions of reality presented in the context of impersonal academic disciplines, there might well be more thought given to the personality of the curriculum, counterbalancing the current impersonality.

In higher education today knowledge is organized around academic disciplines. This organization has a special relevance for scholars and researchers and it is certainly not irrelevant for ordinary students. It is nevertheless a clerical organization of knowledge which serves most directly the interests of the academic priesthood. There are, of course, good explanations for its predominance. The expansion of knowledge has come largely through research, which is conducted by people who have become specialists in their particular academic disciplines. The national importance of research and technical expertise in our society is reflected in the growth of the graduate school. Both as the training ground for future researchers, and as the locus of current researchers, the graduate school is quite properly organized to enhance the potential of the academic disciplines—their concepts, theories, and methods of inquiry. Since entrance into college teaching comes by way of training in the graduate school, it is perhaps not surprising that the typical organization of subject matter in the graduate school has become the typical organization of subject matter in the undergraduate curriculum as well. Moreover, since an increasing number of college graduates are entering graduate school, knowledge organized around academic disciplines is obviously relevant in their undergraduate training.

The emphasis on academic disciplines is also the main characteristic of the current curriculum reform movement in the elementary and secondary schools. John Goodlad has recently written a critical analysis of this movement.

[Its] objectives . . . stress the importance of understanding the structure of the discipline, the purposes and methods of the field, and the part that creative men and women played in developing the field.[2]

The current curriculum reform movement is partly a reaction to perceived curricular excesses of the 30's and 40's. To the extent that this reaction to child-centered and society-oriented theories is itself perceived to be an overemphasis on subject matter in determining curricular ends and means, today's movement already is breeding tomorrow's counter-reaction. But today's movement is also a response to the problems created by vast accumulations of knowledge and new ways of structuring it, so that men engage more effectively in the pursuit of knowledge.[3]

In collegiate education in the 1930's and 1940's there was much discussion and much activity around the topic of "general education." This was partly a response to what many educators described as "overspecialization." Chicago developed survey courses. Minnesota's General College developed a set of orientation courses dealing with problems of vocation, home and family, personal adjustment, and current affairs. Columbia had a course called Contemporary Civilization. Syracuse developed a course called Responsible Citizenship. Wisconsin's experimental college focused on the study of Greek and Roman civilizations. Harvard inaugurated a general education program. Although the general education label is seldom used today, and although many of these earlier enterprises have disappeared, the problem has not vanished. And there is, indeed, the beginning of a counter-reaction to the dominance of the academic disciplines and their abstract impersonality. One of the newest efforts to give more personal meaning to undergraduate teaching at Berkeley is a program very similar in conception to the experimental college which flourished at Wisconsin more than thirty years ago.

I have suggested that the academic disciplines represent a clerical organization of knowledge. This mode of organization is one which all students should encounter and should come to understand and value to the best of their ability. But however essential and necessary we believe it to be, it is not a sufficient organization of knowledge. In the college curriculum there must also be opportunities for systematic encounter with secular organizations of knowledge. What I mean here is knowledge brought to bear directly on topics and problems of broad societal and personal concern—problems of citizenship, morality, conservation, survival, justice, freedom, authority, self-understanding, communication,

[2] John I. Goodlad, *School Curriculum Reform in the United States* (New York: The Fund for the Advancement of Education, 1964), p. 54.
[3] *Ibid.*, p. 87.

creativity. These are abstract topics, too, as abstract as those within the academic disciplines; but they are not impersonal, for they clearly demand personal and collective decisions which affect all our lives. It is because of this personal relevance that I have used the expression "the personality of the curriculum" to suggest one new concept for thinking about institutional goals for students.

In psychology, when we talk about personality we mean the pattern and style in which the accumulated experience of the individual is stored, evaluated, and expressed. In a sense, it is the absorption of personal meaning from the events that have confronted the human organism. When there are events beyond the immediate capacity of the organism to absorb, or events to which no personal meaning can be attached, the personality or ego regresses to a lower or more primitive level of adaptation. And so it is with a student faced with an impersonal and, to him, implacable set of curriculum demands for verbal abstraction and memorization of technical terminology; he can attach no real personal meaning to such demands for the simple reason that they are irrelevant to his past, present, and anticipated future. Such a person may be quite intelligent and, indeed, quite intellectual in the sense of having a genuine curiosity about the meaning of his life and the society in which it is being lived, but the impact of the curriculum upon him is nevertheless similar to the phenomenon of regression, for it induces a devaluing of the academic or clerical concept of intellectuality without providing any comparably valued secular concept of intellectuality to sustain or reward him. Thus, paradoxically, the curricular emphasis on the academic disciplines produces, in some students, an anti-intellectualism or, in short, the opposite of what the emphasis is intended to produce. If one thinks seriously about the personality of the curriculum, which really means its perceived relevance to the variety of learners for whom it is intended, then the balance between clerical and secular organizations of knowledge becomes a potentially critical factor in the cognitive as well as the affective development of the students.

A second new concept in institutional goals for students is the concept of public service. It is a fact that many students are involved in the civil rights movement—they are actively concerned with the right of all people to the use of public accommodations, to justice and equal protection under the law, with the right of all people to register and vote, to buy a house, and to attend school with a reasonably broad segment of the human race instead of with an insulated segment. It is a fact that many students have been attracted to and have served in the Peace Corps. It is a fact that many students are interested in the so-called poverty programs; in working for the Job Corps; or in VISTA, the domestic counterpart of the Peace Corps; or in project Headstart. It is a fact that many students in schools of education have shown a new interest in the prospect of teaching school in depressed areas. It is a fact that volunteer projects such as tutoring children in slum areas and raising money to send children to summer camps are common on many college campuses. To the best of my knowledge, it is also a fact that there is no recognition or reward for any of these public service activities on any college campus in the United States. By recognition I mean any official acknowledgment that such public services are relevant to the objectives of higher education and therefore to be counted toward the fulfillment of requirements for graduation.

Public service is an institutional goal—but not for students! For them is is more likely to be a risk—a risk of academic failure and institutional displeasure. It is significant that the active leaders of last year's Free Speech Movement at Berkeley were among the brightest students on the Berkeley campus, students whose intellectual aptitudes were so high that they could afford the time and still make high grades in their courses.

There are, of course, limits to social and political activism. The body politic can be pushed but it cannot be inflamed. I am not suggesting that students be given academic credit for trying to reform the world. I am suggesting, however, that there is a vast social laboratory which needs to be used to enrich the study of society. We teach courses *about* government, *about* sociology, or *about* art; but we teach courses *in* chemistry. To read about chemistry is not enough; the student must also do chemistry. He must mix, measure, filtrate, test. We take for granted that the laboratory experience is essential to an understanding of the subject. It is in this laboratory sense that I believe something approaching public service as an institutional goal for students can be realized,

Among many students there is a desire for commitment and involvement. Perhaps to a greater extent than we have appreciated, some of this desire can be recognized and rewarded through laboratory work in the relevant parts of the college curriculum.

As a third new concept in institutional goals for students, we need a new concept of the individuality of higher education that is compatible with the individuality of learning and development. For the institution, education is a group enterprise; for the student, it is an individual enterprise. This difference in concept presents a fascinating paradox: the more education is sought by the masses, the less applicable are mass methods of providing it. As greater numbers of students enroll in colleges and universities—and already more than half of the nation's high school graduates are going on to college—the result is greater heterogeneity in the talents, backgrounds, and aspirations of the student bodies of most institutions. As a consequence of this heterogeneity no one massive technique and no one homogeneous curriculum are any longer suitable. There must be more differentiation and more individualization in order to reach large numbers effectively.

What does a concept of the individuality of higher education suggest? For the administration it suggests a role that places more emphasis on the management of diversity and less emphasis on the enforcement of common standards. For the faculty it suggests more emphasis on variety and innovation in teaching modes, more recognition and reward for a variety of student talents, and less emphasis on common curricula and common requirements for graduation. For the students it suggests more opportunity for choice and for success, and less demand for conformity to a single standard.

The single standard is a big part of the problem. Five or six generations ago the ordinary college student could, in five or six hours a week, prepare all his lessons. Even though the lessons were dull and irrelevant to the lives of most students, they could be mastered without too much demand on the students' time, leaving ample opportunity for participation in the debating societies and other aspects of the extracurriculum which, for the most part, students had invented to bring a greater degree of intellectual vitality and personal relevance to their college years. In those days, the student body was considerably more homogeneous than it is today in respect to social, economic, and cultural status, although there was, as there is today, a considerable range of aptitude for abstract, intellectual pursuits. Besides, the development of character was regarded as more fundamentally important than the development of intellect, and the time spent in chapel was as rigidly prescribed as the time spent in the classroom. But the time formerly required by both the curriculum and the extracurriculum was not as great as the time that the present-day average student must devote to the single goal of mastering, or at least passing, a succession of courses in the academic disciplines. And today the avenues of escape from this confrontation with academic disciplines are rapidly closing.

If it were true that academic aptitude and academic performance possess some general quality of goodness that is basic to other valued attributes, the concentration on them might be more defensible, but unfortunately they possess no such general virtue. Academic potential and academic grades are related to one another, but neither has any relationship to other measures of competence and achievement. In a recent study by the American College Testing Program, it was found that when academic aptitude scores and high school grades were each correlated with a series of other achievements and competencies all the correlations turned out to be approximately zero.[4] There just is not any connection between academic potential or performance, on the one hand, and artistic, scientific, and social accomplishment, on the other—not with arts achievement, literary achievement, musical achievement, science achievement, leadership achievement, nor with technical competence, business and clerical competence, arts competencies, leadership competencies, foreign language competency, or interpersonal competency. Moreover, in another recent report from the American College Testing Program, some fifty or more studies relating college grades to various measures of adult success were reviewed; and again, the results were almost totally negative.[5] This is not to say that grades are worthless or that they are in any sense invalid; it is to say, however, that they have little or no relationship with any other personally and socially valued achievements. Apparently they exist in rather lonely isolation from the rest of the world. However, it is with the rest of the world that today's students are seeking, and in some places demanding, a greater connection.

No one would quarrel with a demand for excellence in student performance. But when excellence has only one definition (high grades) and when this definition has no relationship with other kinds of excellence, then it does seem to me that we have lost contact rather badly between our concept of education and the individuality of our students.

A concept of the individuality of higher education compatible with the individuality of students can be exemplified in three ways: by greater flexibility in the choice, the timing, and the sequencing of what is studied; by greater variety in the kinds of talent and performance that are officially rewarded; and by greater diversity in the ways in which teaching and learning are carried out.

The potential for greater diversity in the modes of teaching and learning has been significantly enhanced by technology—recordings, video tapes, teaching machines, and other sorts of programmed learning —and by other familiar innovations such as independent study programs, panel discussions, group projects, team teaching, field trips, and so on. In so far as these represent opportunities for students to learn through various kinds of stimuli and thus depart from a single mode of learning, they reflect some acknowledgment of the diversity of learners. In so far as they deal only with the time that may be required for learning, as in programmed instruction, they represent a more efficient sub-

[4] John L. Holland and James M. Richards, Jr., "Academic and Non-Academic Accomplishment: Correlated or Uncorrelated?," ACT Research Reports No. 2 (Iowa City: American College Testing Program, April 1965).

[5] Donald P. Hoyt, "The Relationship Between College Grades and Adult Achievement: A Review of the Literature," ACT Research Reports No. 7 (Iowa City: American College Testing Program, September 1965).

stitute for the generally discarded and wasteful practice of making a student repeat a grade or a course until he can pass it.

As to giving recognition to a greater variety of talent and performance, I would merely urge that it be done. Is the ability to analyze and describe on paper, with skill and subtlety, the complexity of some literary character more significant than the ability to project and portray this character through skill and subtlety of action on the stage? Is the ability to criticize some old or new way of life in a philosophical essay more important than the ability to exemplify it in a painting or a piece of sculpture? Is the ability to define what sociologists mean by socio-economic status more important than the ability to establish rapport with, and successfully assist and encourage, a little slum girl and her parents? In higher education today the answer to all these questions is "yes"; but perhaps the answer in each case should be that both abilities are important.

As to providing more flexibility in the curriculum—in the choice, timing, and sequencing of what is studied—I do not suggest reverting to a free choice, help yourself, smorgasbord of academic goodies. But I do think we need to examine afresh why a writer or a housewife has to take a course in mathematics or chemistry but a mathematician or chemist does not have to take a course in Shakespeare or painting, or why English composition has to be taken before English literature. Basically, if higher education is to serve a diversity of students, then it needs to be defined and presented in ways sufficiently diverse to enable each student to find meaning and value in the combination of courses that constitute his curriculum. And thus we come full circle to the paradox stated earlier: The more education is sought by the masses, the less effective are mass methods of providing it.

A fourth concept in institutional goals for students, and the capstone for all others, is a concept of the college itself as an honest exemplar of its own goals. Is the college, in its policies and procedures, in its administrative and academic practices, in its teaching, research, and public services, an example of the values and goals it means to set before its students?

Over the past few years some two hundred or more colleges and universities have given to a sample of their upperclassmen a test of mine called *College & University Environment Scales*.[6] The test consists of a list of 150 statements about the college environment—that is, statements about policies, events, conditions, activities, attitudes, and so on —that may be generally true of some colleges but not true of others. When students agree, by a consensus of two to one or greater, in their

[6] C. Robert Pace, *College & University Environment Scales* (Princeton, New Jersey: Educational Testing Service, 1962).

responses to a particular statement, then that statement is regarded as being characteristic of the college. It is, in other words, something which is collectively perceived to be true about the environment by those who live in it. One can think of the results as a photograph of the campus showing what features are most clearly reflected. As in any portrait, the subject does not always like what the photographer produces.

In a few colleges an interesting variation in the use of these scales has been tried. Having discovered what the students perceive to be characteristic of the campus environment, the college has then taken another cross-section of students, and a cross-section of the faculty, and asked them to respond to the statements from a different perspective, one which reflects the ideal rather than the actual. If this college were ideal, that is, the kind of place you would want it to be, would this statement be true about it? Each statement is then answered from this ideal perspective. The collective ideal can then be compared with the collectively perceived reality. The discrepancies are suggestive of how clearly the actual environment is an exemplar of the ideals and values its members believe it ought to exemplify. In the places where such comparisons have been made, some major discrepancies have been revealed. To the extent that the college itself is an honest exemplar of its own goals, its potential impact on the growth and development of its students is thereby enhanced.

I have tried to suggest, in this brief essay, four concepts which seem to me relevant to current thinking about institutional goals for students—the personality of the curriculum; public service; the individuality and diversity of learning, development, and talent; and the institution itself as an exemplar of its ideals. I would wish for college students today encounters with both clerical and secular organizations of knowledge, encouragement of and recognition for the acquisition and expression of understanding in a variety of ways, opportunity for the development of value commitments through participation and public service, and four years of experience in an institution where these goals are exemplified with clarity, style, and compassion.

Landrum R. Bolling

RELATING THE ADMINISTRATION TO THE INDIVIDUAL STUDENT

As I THOUGHT ABOUT PRESENTING THIS PAPER, IT SEEMED THAT WHAT I most wanted to do was primarily to talk about some of the great central issues of educational philosophy and about some of the important roles that the college president has to play if his institution is to be significant and if it is to accomplish the kind of purposes in general and for students that we say should be accomplished. Along the way I hope I shall have something to say about my topic of Relating the Administration to the Individual Student. So much for these words of introduction.

Last week a friend of mine who is a president of a college similar to those represented here at this Conference told me of a dream, a nightmare, he had had just two nights before. He dreamed that he had come back from a typical, inescapable college business trip to find his desk piled high with typical, inescapable mountains of paper. As he sat down to his work he became aware of a delegation of students standing on the other side of the desk and obviously wanting to talk to him. In his dream this college president tried to reach across to shake hands but he found that he could not stretch that high and that far. He tried to shove the papers aside and reach through the canyon walls but the papers kept landsliding in on him as he dug into them with his hands. Slowly the mountain of papers rose higher and higher until the students completely disappeared from view and, discouraged, quietly slipped away. That true dream of a real college president—and I might say, this concerns a relatively small, church-related college, not some gigantic multiversity—that dream, I suspect, is symbolic of the experiences of most of us, or at least of the fears that at times haunt us. We may never have to face a Berkeley style student-administration

48

confrontation of physical intimidation, police action, and noncommunicating bitterness, but we all share a certain anxiety and a certain guilt about the relation between the administration and the students. We all hope that around the corner there will be found the time, the imagination, the wisdom, the patience, the courage, and the mutual understanding to put our student-administration relations on a basis nearer to our heart's desire. We hope that we may be able to relate the administration of our colleges more effectively to the individual student whose emotional, intellectual, and general welfare must be our primary concern, whose growth and development are our reasons for being. No college administrator (I am sure this goes without saying) can claim to have a firm sense of how best to deal with these intensely human problems. No two colleges or universities are made up of quite the same mix of people and problems; and the flowing stream of change moves so swiftly across the social landscape and through our campuses that what may have seemed a suitable answer yesterday is not adequate today and will surely not be good enough tomorrow. Whatever is said about this subject must be said with some caution, some tentativeness, and will inevitably reflect personal and partial experience. What may be most worth saying may be certain admissions of mistakes in the past, certain affirmations of hope for the future, and certain reflections on the unavoidable conflicts between the young and the old, and on the inevitable responsibilities and frustrations of power.

Those who are charged with the central administrative tasks in an educational institution must always realize that theirs is an essentially lonely work and that for the most effective handling of this work they cannot behave like competitors in a popularity contest. They will not be able to make everybody happy, certainly not everyone connected with the institution who also belongs to the age group of the late adolescent. It is part of the teen-age subculture and of the psychological needs of individual young persons to challenge authority and to protest controls and restraints. This is in the nature of things, as we all know. This is certainly true of those who are bright, eager, and aggressive as are most of today's college students, whose lives and attitudes have been conditioned by the sweeping changes of this era. We live in a time, as David Riesman has put it, when there is more than a generation's difference between the generations. We have to live with differences of viewpoints and interests. We have to accept a certain tension as normal. This means, among other things, that we as administrators should not be greatly surprised by anything that our students want or say or do, and we should try insofar as is possible to refuse to allow ourselves to be upset by their behavior, although I am sure that on occasion the forthright expression of honest indignation toward outrageous language and conduct is right and salutary. Administrative indignation, however, if it is to be effective, must be carefully rationed. More important, the college presidents must approach their relations with students on the basis of believing in them, and searching with them to find the best means for building significant and constructive relations. We can and should try to enjoy our students.

We all probably have heard of at least one case of the unhappy grade-school teacher whose basic problem is that she *cannot stand* children. When we as administrators are least effective with students it is often when our emotional involvement in the conflict with them has become excessive—sometimes to the point where we wish we could get rid of the students or at least of these particular students so we could run the college the way it ought to be run. Admittedly, it is not always easy to enjoy students for not all of them are always enjoyable. Yet without falling into naïve sentimentality we have to act on the belief that it is possible to achieve a high level of essentially harmonious relations between students and administration.

I would like to say here that in my efforts to learn something about this business, and I hope I am at last beginning to learn about this sort of thing, I have found that some of my most rewarding contacts with students have been with those who have been most troublesome and have been most irksome to me—when and if I am able to overcome my irritation and anger to the point where I can sit with them and find out what is really on their minds, and what is really "bugging" them. I sometimes find underneath the surface—underneath their, to me, sometimes exceedingly offensive exteriors (complete with scraggly beards and the rest of it)—that I am able to find a sympathetic kind of human being and someone with whom I can really communicate. The barrier is often in myself because I get put off by the absolutely stupid and absurd things they have said or done on the campus and would really like to write them off without giving them a chance to be heard. It is very instructive to one to have to discipline himself in this way, I think; perhaps we shall be better administrators in the years ahead because we have had to endure some of the things we have had to endure in the last hectic year or two. The fulfillment of the constructive purposes of our educational enterprise, I am sure we all agree, requires, at least to a minimal degree, a certain harmony between students and administration. I believe all of us can lift the level of this relationship if we try hard enough and wisely.

In seeking to build that harmony and in trying to relate the administration positively to the individual student, there are many places to begin and many steps to be taken. I should like to suggest that an important beginning is with the definition of the essential character and personality of the institution and the communicating of that definition to prospective and newly admitted students. Despite all the growing attention given to counseling in the high schools and by the admissions departments of the colleges, too many students arrive on the college campuses each fall with the mistaken notion that they are entering some other kind of college than the real one to which they have been admitted. I drew quite a bit of knowing laughter at the opening convocation at Earlham in September by saying rather bluntly that I was sure that some of the difficulties we had at Earlham resulted from the fact that when some of the students got off the bus in Richmond, Indiana, they thought they had arrived in Yellow Springs, Ohio, and that while I have great admiration for Antioch, Earlham is not a Quaker Antioch. I think this is the kind of problem that we are increasingly facing on the college campuses: making sure that students have some idea in advance of the kind of college they are entering. I certainly agree with what Dr. Pace has said: that as the mass nature of our educational system becomes more evident, greater diversity in our approaches to education and more precise discrimination among the types of institution are required. Many students come to college confused or uncertain about the expectations—intellectual, social, and personal—being set before them. The administration bears a peculiarly important responsibility, working with faculty and trustees, to make a clear definition of the college's general and specific purposes, its standards and values, its policies and regulations, and to see that full and understandable interpretation is continually given to the college's various constituencies and particularly to the prospective students and, each fall, to the whole student body.

This is not to say that the college's identity will not change from time to time. Of course it will change. This is not to say that each student generation will not give something of its own color and tone to the college's identity, nor can we deny to students the right to challenge the college's current identity and to try, in the open market of ideas, to change that definition in significant ways. What I am concerned about is that the college, as an on-going institution, as a community of memory and of hope, shall have some clear sense of what it is and where it is going, what its essential values are, and what expectations it sets for its students. What I am concerned about is that the college, and specifically our type of private, church-related, liberal arts college, not become such a flabby, gelatinous mass that its shape is going to be formed, by default, by the unrelenting pressures from successive generations of students and by capricious forces pushing in upon us from beyond the campus gates. I think that today this is a real danger. We of the small liberal arts colleges know that we cannot be all things to all men. Yet we are so often unclear about our institutional identity that in important ways we confuse at times everybody, including the students. The chief responsibility for dealing with that confusion, I believe, rests squarely on the college president. How does he go about discharging that responsibility?

I should like to suggest that his first duty is to arrive at some inner conviction about what are the peculiar and special qualities of the institution over which he presides. What are the special reasons for its existence? If he has been on the staff for some time he may already have a strong judgment about these matters. If he has newly arrived from the outside, he is obviously going to consult trustees, older faculty members, alumni, and, to be sure, the younger faculty members and students as well, to see if he can discover what substance, if any, lies behind the rhetoric of the catalog which inevitably will claim that this college is truly remarkable and a special kind of place. If his inquiries fail to produce any convincing evidence that the institution currently has any special and peculiar qualities worth struggling to preserve, the president then faces a simple dilemma. He can either recommend that his institution be absorbed by the nearest state university, or he can undertake the considerable task of establishing within the institution those peculiar and special values which he and his trustees and faculty believe to be realistic and proper expectations and for which they will put forth the necessary effort. If he does, in fact, find supporting truth for the claims of unusual and special qualities, or if he is courageous enough to undertake to create the peculiar values hoped for but not yet attained, he then faces the hard, endless, never-to-be-finished and infinitely exciting work of developing, maintaining, and enlivening the educational program and the over-all college community life which will give continuing substance to the aim of peculiar qualities and special values.

Let me say bluntly here that I think this crisis of identity is at the heart of our problems in the small church-related college. I think sentiment and tradition are not enough to sustain us and to justify our continued existence, are not enough to justify all the unusual, extraordinary, and strenuous efforts that must be made to keep these colleges going. However noble the old ideals may have been, and however effective the expression may have been in individual lives, this sort of thing gets eroded in time, and unless there is real substance now, and unless there is a sense of genuine building upon this for the future, I think it is quite right and proper for trustees, for church bodies, and for individual administrative groups to question seriously whether they ought really to try to keep such a college alive, or to keep it operating in its particular pattern. I also would like to say that in the search for institutional identity it is not enough to say that our purpose is "academic excellence," one of the most hackneyed, shopworn clichés of academia in the last ten years. Unless we can come up with a better, more specific definition of our goals than this, I think we really ought to examine the question of whether we have a reason for being.

In my opening statement to the Earlham faculty when I became president in 1958, I said some things that have haunted me ever since because I was not then exactly certain how to make them a reality, and I am not wholly sure now. Taking into account the great concern of our own faculty (and of every other college faculty) for greater academic achievement—greater reality to the dream of academic excellence—I said that of course I wanted Earlham to be excellent, but that to be a great college is *not good enough.* I said that unless we can be a significant college there is no point in making the effort required to try to win this elusive goal of academic excellence. I believed then and I believe now that it is not easy to develop a college that is significant when judged by criteria beyond the usual ones that we so easily get caught up in talking about. But I believe even more than I did then that it lies within our grasp to make our small colleges distinctive, to build into them the best of unusual qualities and characteristics, and to cause them to be truly significant, and significant in terms that go beyond the conventional criteria of "academic excellence."

You may ask what all this has to do with relating the administration to the individual student. As I see it, the crucial problem of most of the private church-related colleges is that of establishing a genuine, meaningful institutional identity and of attracting the students who can and will relate constructively to the institution's basic character and personality. The articulation of that identity is essential to recruiting teachers, to securing financial support, and to recruiting the right kind of students.

Let me say one word here about recruiting teachers. This has come to haunt me more and more. If we are going to build the kind of college I feel we must try to build at Earlham, and to which we give lip service, I am convinced that we are going to have to give much more time to faculty recruiting than we have done in the past. We are going to have to allow ourselves a great deal more lead time in looking for faculty, in trying to spot promising people—on the Danforth list and other lists— in seeing how the young scholars are coming along in graduate schools, in trying to get in touch with them, in trying perhaps to develop internships by which we can "sneak" them into the faculty and help them finish up their graduate work after we get them involved in our institutions. I think we shall have to use a great deal of ingenuity, perseverance, and determination to get the kind of faculty we really want, teachers who share the values and purposes we have been trying to articulate here. Only if we are able to recruit and train and indoctrinate that basic core of faculty members who identify personally with our kind of college and its values will we be able to achieve the kind of over-all institutional purposes that we say we have. But I am convinced that if we are able to do this, that if we are able to articulate these purposes and find these teachers and get them enlisted in developing that kind of college, the financial support will come. I have not the slightest doubt in the world about it. There is plenty of money in this land to support educational programs in which people know where they are going and who they are and what kind of vision of greatness they are prepared to work for—for themselves and for their students.

Recruiting the right kind of students is, of course, another tricky business, both for the students and for the college. Here again, I think, in spite of the ease with which we can all accumulate far more applications than we can accept, the problem becomes more difficult, more complex, not easier than it was when we were simply trying to keep the dormitories filled. Choosing one's college (along with choosing a mate and a career) is one of three great decisions made in a person's life. Most high school seniors should know more about the colleges they are considering than in fact they do. We in the colleges ought to know more about the student than we do. So long as we served primarily the sons and daughters of a particular church group drawn primarily from a quite limited geographical area, this kind of problem was more manageable than it is today. Today our church and alumni constituencies are scattered across the nation, among various social and economic classes, and reflect within themselves a considerable range of values and attitudes. In the competitive scramble for colleges our institutions are being sought out more and more by students and counselors who have never had any association with these institutions, are not traditionally related to our constituencies, and know very little about us. Meanwhile, we at the colleges have greatly broadened our recruiting efforts. Moreover, with the rising flood of applications and the growing faculty concern for stricter attention to evidences of academic preparation and aptitude, all institutions are moving toward a greater emphasis on intellectual competence as the prime criterion for admission. This tends to move us farther and farther away from our own traditional constituencies and from the previously accepted values and attitudes of those constituencies. For the church-related colleges this means almost inevitably an increasing secularization, a watering down of its Christian witness, a silent and sometimes not so silent erosion of its social and moral standards, plus a weakening of any meaningful

sense of community. Let me say just a word here about the tendency
to up the intellectual standards for admission. We do not really know,
I think, what kinds of persons are going to turn out to be most effective
citizens or professional persons, not even within the academic world.
Even within the narrow criterion of academic performance—and, as
Dr. Pace pointed out, this is not necessarily the most important criterion
—even within this framework, the traditional standards of evaluation
are not terribly precise and it is a bit shocking to think about the cavalier
attitude with which we deal with our prospective students.

I was speaking a moment ago about the changes in our institutional
character, increasing secularization, and so on, and I should like to go
on to say that not all these changes are necessarily bad. The church
leaders have long been saying that the church must live in this world
and must try to change the world. This is certainly the call of the church-
related college. Much of what we are moving away from was parochial,
formalistic, even stultifying and hollow. But what are we moving toward? What new reformulated institutional purpose are we adopting and
to what extent is that emerging definition a result of deliberate thought
and explicit choices by the faculty, the administration, and the board of
trustees, and to what extent are our significant changes of institutional
identity the haphazard results of accumulated student pressures and the
blind social forces of our time? It may not be a necessarily shocking
and antidemocratic idea to suggest that the fortuitous and heterogeneous
collection of young people, whose ages are between seventeen and
twenty-two, and who occupy the dormitories for a maximum of four
years, have no necessarily superior claim to exercise the dominant
voice in determining institutional identity and in certain important areas
forcing into effect basic changes in college policies.

(Let me put in parenthetically, though, that this may be one of the
many options we ought to hold open in our pluralistic American system
of higher education. This is what to a degree obtained in the medieval
centers of learning. It is what may be developing in a semi-underground
way on the fringes of our larger universities today. The student-domi-
nated college as an experimental alternative perhaps ought to be tried,
if only some of our eager, ambitious, rebellious, and daring young men
would recruit some teachers, get themselves a grant, and begin. But
that is perhaps a far-out notion that has no relevance to the real problems we are dealing with today.)

What I want to say is that nature and college students abhor a
vacuum. If it is not filled in one way, it will be in another. If the older
and more permanent members of the college community do not give
clear guidelines, a set of standards and values, the students will. They
will try in any case. And here inevitably come the trouble and tension.

What I fear is happening on many college campuses today is that the faculty and administration are no longer very clear about what kind of an institution they want to be, or what kind they think it is intellectually and socially respectable to try to be. Hence, they are caught up in an exercise of giving ground inch by inch under the pressure of student demands for change toward something they have not thought through very well either. The answer to all this, I submit, is to be found neither in supine submission nor in laying down the law from on high. What I want to make a plea for can be summarized in the following points:

First, the president and his administrative colleagues need to exercise initiative and leadership in rearticulating the basic purposes, philosophy, and peculiar standards and values of the institution. This need not be a mere echo of past pronouncements. Yet, inasmuch as colleges are living organisms with roots in the past, any rearticulation of identity must make significant recognition that a tradition does in fact exist. Insofar as important departures from tradition may be called for by a thoughtful analysis of current needs of the younger generation and of their times, the administration and faculty should take the lead in bringing those changes about. They should use all their wit and wisdom to avoid falling into a pattern of recurring, disorganized retreat. They should hold aloft a banner of positive purposes relevant to the needs of our day. Here I would like to underscore again what some of us were saying in the discussion this morning. In the area of academic change, the administration and the students often have common perceptions of the problem, common interests in the types of changes they ought to work for, and I believe it is important that the faculty and the administration enter into a dialogue with the students about the nature of the academic enterprise and draw from students their best insights of how this enterprise can be improved. I would not take as one hundred per cent wisdom everything they would suggest, but as the consumers of what we purvey, they have a legitimate right to express some judgments about it.

Second, the president and his colleagues must pay particular attention to those nonclassroom activities, events, and experiences which promote a lively intercourse among the disciplines and bring together the students, the faculty, and the administration, and which build bridges between the arts and the sciences, between the recreational and the academic, between the intellectual and the spiritual. The president may not get much chance to teach classes or to prescribe a course of study but he has extraordinary opportunities still on most of our campuses to influence the development of the cocurricular and the extramural life of the campus. He can do much to set the tone and guide the thrust of campus religious life, to broaden the scope of the recreational activities, particularly those which bring the students into contact with the older members of the academic community, and to promote the all-college programs for the performing arts and for public lectures in a variety of fields. What is done in this broad area of campus life is of inestimable value in establishing the over-all character of the institution. I realize that traditionally the extracurricular activities have largely grown up in a fairly unplanned and spontaneous way, chiefly under student leadership, to fill gaps in their time and to enable them to satisfy intellectual and artistic interests that may not be satisfied by the regular curriculum. I also realize that it is dangerous to overstructure this area of the college. It would be too bad if we shut off opportunities for student spontaneity. But I so strongly believe that the extracurricular is basically so important to the total college experience that I think the college administration needs to give it more attention and care and to assign to it much more in the budget than most of us have in the past been willing to do. It is in this area that so often the real ethos of the institution is determined. The real climate, the real atmosphere, of the institution may be determined by what happens outside the classroom rather than in what the faculty and students do and say to one another in the fifty-minute class periods. It is in this extramural life of the college that the president, I think, still has an important role to play and, if not the president directly, certainly his administrative colleagues.

Third, the president and his administrative colleagues have the opportunity and the responsibility to set the tone of the day-by-day personal human relations on campus. Their ways of dealing with people will be reflected in the pattern of personal relations on the campus. They will, through their daily words and deeds, communicate more effectively than fine phrases in the catalog a spirit of straightforwardness or of deviousness, of openness or of concealment, of trustfulness or of suspicion, of good will or of hostility. The style of the administration will in considerable measure set the style of the college community, whether of bureaucratic niggling or of practical concern for fairness and reasonableness, whether of flabby indecision or of firmness and clarity. The college will be seen to exist either for the purpose of doing its institutional housekeeping in the most tidy manner or for promoting the most creative growth of its students. Valuable and essential as they are, the business manager and the registrar, as Henry Wriston has pointedly reminded us, have necessarily only a partial view of the institution. They and their rules and regulations must not always be the final word. And I might add that the president must see to it that the faculty does not hide behind these administrative officers and their procedures to avoid making difficult but vital decisions for which the faculty ultimately has the final responsibility. Basically, the registrar is there to carry out the rules of the faculty.

Fourth, the president and his administrative colleagues and the faculty must keep before the students, and attempt to communicate to the outer constituencies, a fresh and renewed vision of what the college educational experience at its best can be and ought to be. Upon us rests the responsibility for raising the expectations of a college education:

above the passing of courses, beyond the acquiring of information, beyond the earning of grades, beyond the winning of honors and of degrees. We shall inevitably increase the size and difficulty of our work if we raise those expectations. But only such a mission is worthy of our best efforts. Only as we work at that task can we really relate ourselves to the fundamental needs and the potentialities of our students.

Almost one hundred years ago, Francis Parkman, then a Harvard Overseer, wrote a little essay for *The Nation* in which he called for reaffirmation of the purposes of education so that education can be directed "not to stuffing the mind with the crude aggregations of imperfect knowledge, but rather to the development of its powers of observation, comparison, analysis, and reasoning; to strengthening and instructing its moral sense, and leading it to self-knowledge and consequent modesty."[1] His words have a striking freshness and import for education in our day. What we are called to do, certainly in our church-related colleges if they are to survive, is to build vital, vigorous, creative, and concerned communities of faith and learning and to initiate young people into the life of that community. Is not that the real question before us? Certainly the question is *not* how best to keep the student happy, well behaved, adjusted, and responsible to administrative desires and demands.

In his Columbia University Bicentennial Address in 1954, Dr. J. Robert Oppenheimer had some perceptive observations on this concept of the community of learning:

> . . . The problem of the scientist is . . . not different from that of the artist or of the historian. He needs to be a part of the community, and the community can only with loss and peril be without him. . . . For a university rightly and inherently is a place where the individual man can form new syntheses, where the accidents of friendship and association can open a man's eyes to a part of science or art which he had not known before, where parts of human life, remote and perhaps superficially incompatible, can find in men their harmony and their synthesis.[2]

One of the tragedies of our education is that so often we will not allow time and room to examine the perhaps superficial and incompatible. Yet with clear realism, Dr. Oppenheimer went on to point out how difficult it is to hold together in this time of exploding knowledge and specialization a real community of learning.

[1] Francis Parkman, "The Tale of the 'Ripe Scholar,'" *The Nation,* IX: 234 (Dec. 23, 1869), pp. 560 ff.
[2] J. Robert Oppenheimer, "Prospects in the Arts and Sciences," *Man's Right to Knowledge* (Second Series; New York: Herbert Muschel, 1954), p. 112.

For the truth is that this is indeed, inevitably and increasingly, an open and, inevitably and increasingly, an eclectic world. We know too much for one man to know much. We live too variously to live as one. . . . Our knowledge separates as well as it unites. . . . The artist's loneliness, the scholar despairing, because no one will any longer trouble to learn what he can teach, the narrowness of the scientist— these are not unnatural insignia in this great time of change. . . .

This is a world in which each of us, knowing his limitations, knowing the evils of superficiality and the terrors of fatigue, will have to cling to what is close to him, to what he knows, to what he can do, to his friends and his tradition and his love, lest he be dissolved in a universal confusion and know nothing and love nothing. . . .

This cannot be an easy life. We shall have a rugged time of it to keep our minds open and to keep them deep, to keep our sense of beauty and our ability to make it, and our occasional ability to see it in places remote and strange and unfamiliar. . . . But this, as I see it, is the condition of man; and in this condition we can help, because we can love, one another.[3]

When I first read those words it was difficult for me to think of them as coming from a great, aloof physical scientist and as being spoken in the setting of a vast university, but never mind. They speak particularly to the opportunities, the needs, the responsibilities of the church-related liberal arts college.

Now let me get back to a final word on this theme of relating the administration to the individual student. What is important about that relationship is not the technique of communication or the struggle over rules and regulations or even the skills of personal counseling. What is important is a shared vision and a shared experience of a community of learning, which even in this secular age can and should be a community of both faith and learning. The articulating of that concept of community is the special responsibility of the administration.

To build, to sustain, and to nurture that kind of community is the obligation which should outweigh all the other duties of the president and his administrative colleagues. Unless the president is willing to accept that burden, I quite honestly believe the job will not be done. If the administration does not have that vision and commitment, the kind of community I am talking about will not flourish. If there is this vision and commitment, they will inform and illumine all relationships involving administration, faculty, and students within the college. Such a community, of course, cannot be created by administrative fiat. Its creation will require the labor of teachers and administrators and students. Here is where the relations between students, faculty, and ad-

[3] Oppenheimer, *op. cit.,* pp. 113–115.

ministration can be elevated above petty bickering and suspicion and mutual hostility. I do not believe we have begun to tap the reservoirs of talent, energy, and drive that lie within our students for helping to build this kind of community. Whitehead said it long ago. There can be no education really worthy of our best efforts "apart from the habitual vision of greatness." That vision relates clearly not just to personal achievement, fame, fortune, grades, degrees, honors. It relates to constructive creative membership in the great community. Students, I am convinced, respond to that kind of vision once it is clearly presented to them by men and women who believe in such a vision and are committed to helping young people bring it about.

Robert J. Solomon

THE FORWARD LOOK IN TESTING STUDENTS

A FORWARD LOOK IN TESTING MUST OF NECESSITY BE BASED ON A LOOK forward in education—for our purposes, in higher education. Testing is one of the means the educational community may employ to fulfill certain of its objectives or to solve certain of its problems. Therefore, to forecast the developments in testing for higher education requires an appraisal of the trends that are developing in higher education today.

The title of this paper might have been "A Look Forward in Testing Students," but this would not have had quite the same meaning. Whether developments in testing for higher education result in a "forward look" will depend on whether these developments serve the evolving needs of the colleges, their faculties, and their students.

The success of testing, with its prevalence in the United States today, stems from its value to a utilitarian society that accepts social change and believes in human progress, and that is devoted to the identification and development of individual talent as a pathway to progress. As the educational scene changes, a forward look for testing will depend on its ability to continue to be a useful tool. The current trends in higher education suggest that, as the colleges face new challenges to the fulfillment of their responsibilities to the individual student, testing can become more useful and more widely used than it is today.

The form, structure, and content of higher education is changing rapidly, perhaps more rapidly than any other level of education at the present time. By outlining these changes, we can begin to see the shape of things to come for testing.

These changes begin with a redefinition of who and how many go to college. Four mutually reinforcing trends are acting to bring about a dramatic change in the size and composition of the college-bound population. First, the absolute number of individuals of college age has increased dramatically and, despite a decreasing birth rate, the absolute number of births per year will probably continue to increase. Second, the historical trend has been for more students to stay in school longer and for an increasing proportion of them to graduate from high school and become eligible for college. Moreover, as a society we are presently taking additional measures to reduce high school dropouts. Third, there have been, and there will probably continue to be, formidable social forces encouraging an increasing proportion of our high school graduates to go on to college. And, finally, there are growing indications that an increasing proportion of those who either do not go to college immediately after high school graduation, or do not complete college in the conventional manner, will be encouraged to seek ways to obtain and complete a college education. It is not farfetched to conclude that within a generation more than 80 per cent of those who complete high school will go on to some sort of college education, which will probably mean that the colleges will need to provide for more than twice as many undergraduates as they provide for today.

The change in the size of the college-bound population will also be accompanied by a change in its composition. In general, the democratization of the college student body, which has been developing apace with the democratization of American society, will bring to the colleges an ever-increasing proportion of students whose cultural backgrounds, abilities, and interests may be different from those of the prevailing college student body. And, at least in some institutions, there will also be an increasing proportion of returning students whose educations were interrupted for reasons of motivation, money, matrimony, and so forth.

In addition, the structure and organization of higher education is changing. The model of the middle-class student, who on graduation from high school in June goes on to a college the next September and four Junes later receives his baccalaureate from that college, was probably always less than universally accurate, and it is likely to become even less accurate in the future. At least two factors seem to account for this, although statistics are hard to come by for the second factor. The first factor is the growth of the junior and community colleges. Although today these institutions account for a distinct minority of all college students, many of whom do not go on to the last two years of college, within the foreseeable future we may expect that half of all college freshmen will enroll in a junior or community college and that these institutions will provide the four-year institutions with a very significant share of those who are awarded the baccalaureate degree. The second factor, for which scant data are available, is that the institutional mobility of college students appears to be on the increase. There seems to be a growth in the phenomenon of the transfer student, not only from two-year to four-year institutions as might be expected with the increase of two-year colleges, but also from one four-year institution to another. In addition, we have no accurate estimates as to how many of the so-called college dropouts would be better classified as transfer students who move from one institution to another after a relatively brief interruption in their education.

On the college campuses themselves changes are taking place that in the long run may be the most important changes of all. Although the question, "What is a college education?" is hardly a new one, several developments are giving new force to the question today. The staggering increase in the college population and the attendant need to expand college facilities have forced a re-examination of the assumption that the traditional form of instruction is the best form, or that a college degree need be the sum of so many credits for so many hours spent in classrooms, laboratories, and lecture halls. The expansion of community colleges and junior colleges has added impetus to the ever-expanding universe of college-level subjects and curricula. In the last decade, the movements to improve radically the quality and content of the elementary and secondary school curricula have probably increased the differences in the levels and variety of learning that beginning students bring to college and have produced some college students so able that some colleges are finding it difficult to adapt to them. Finally, the values, both intellectual and social, that we now place on a college education have inevitably led the thoughtful and the skeptical to ask questions about the real impact of college on the student; they have been led not merely to ask whether and how college affects the immediate knowledge or eventual income of the students who pass through it, but to inquire as to whether and how a college can really create for each of its students an environment that will foster the development of those desirable intellectual, spiritual, and personal values that are the traditionally accepted outcomes of a college education. As college-going becomes more important for more people, as colleges become more numerous, larger, and more complex, and as college students become more diverse and more accomplished intellectually, the questions, *Why college?* and *Why this college?* will probably be asked with increasing frequency and persistence.

Given this catalog of changes, the question is how will testing help the colleges meet their responsibility to the individual student, a student who obviously has many faces and many ages? What innovations or adaptations will the forward look in testing encompass? What changes may be expected?

Many of the following changes are likely to develop concurrently. But, since our concern is with the individual student, it seems logical to consider these changes in the order in which they will affect him in his educational odyssey.

For the college-bound, we can look forward to a shift of emphasis in testing from the present concern with the *selection* of individuals for college to a greater concern with the *classification* of individuals for college. As the question becomes less one of who goes to college and increasingly one of where one goes and why one goes, the guidance and placement of individuals in terms of their interests and talents will grow in importance. As the size and, more significantly, the composition of the college-bound population change, testing will need to measure the increased diversity of abilities and backgrounds represented in the college-bound population. And, as the number and kinds of colleges increase, testing will need to provide information that will help the individual match his interests, ambitions, and abilities with the institutions and the courses of study that seem best for him. Undoubtedly, there will continue to be a demand for selection testing. If the expansion of our college facilities does not keep pace with the expansion of our college-bound population, selection testing per se may increase in importance. But this seems highly unlikely, and it would have infortunate social and educational consequences. It is more likely that college facilities will be expanded to provide a place for every high school graduate who wishes to go to college and that testing for college, as we know it, will change to meet the new situation.

In one sense, the change may be less radical than it now appears. The fact is that, given sufficient motivation and money, every high school graduate today can find a place in college, although it may not be in the college of his choice. Nevertheless, our attention to date has been focused much more on the academically superior students who traditionally have been considered college material. As the proportion of these students in the total college-bound population decreases, as the college-bound become more numerous and more diverse, and as our definition of who may profit from a college education expands, classification will become more important than selection.

Steps to study such changes are now being considered by the most powerful and prestigious of the organizations that test for college entrance, the College Entrance Examination Board. The College Board is planning to appoint in the near future a commission to review and consider the revision of its testing program in the light of the changes that are now taking place at the college entrance level.

At the recent annual meeting of the College Board, its president, Richard Pearson, explained the need for the commission as follows:

We are moving from an era of scarcity in college admission to one of abundance of educational opportunity. Our future tasks will not be to select a relatively small proportion for college attendance, but, rather, to bring about a broad distribution of students among the variety of opportunities open to them. In these circumstances, we will need to broaden greatly our descriptions of student performance and potential in order that each boy or girl may put forth whatever positive qualifications he may have for a particular college opportunity.

These considerations suggest that the Board should undertake a thoroughgoing and penetrating appraisal of the existing guidance and admission tests in terms of the likely future pressures on the admission scene. The issue is not whether the tests are adequate for today's needs, for we believe that they are. The issue is whether the tests will be adequate for the needs of five to ten years hence, when the cumulation of continued change in the characteristics of the college-going population and in the academic programs of schools and colleges may alter circumstances considerably from what maintains today.

Without attempting to predict the changes that the College Board's commission may recommend, we can make some guesses as to developments that may be considered in the next few years by the College Board or by others. First, we can expect earlier testing and better-articulated testing so that the information available to the student, his parents, and his school, can help him make the right decisions about his educational future early enough and accurately enough to avoid the waste that comes from talent and energy misspent and misdirected. This will probably mean not more time devoted to testing in the schools, but better use of the time now spent and better use of the results.

Also, we may expect the expansion and the improved organization and communication of the information about colleges that will help students to identify those institutions whose academic and social environments seem to match their ability, academic and social interests, and educational plans and objectives. For example, we may expect that in the not-too-distant future, college-bound high school students will be given, in addition to tests of academic ability, elaborate and carefully designed questionnaires that measure the nature and strength of their educational interests, plans, and ambitions, as well as their intellectual and social needs in college.

By relating this information for each student to detailed data that each college would provide as to its academic and social characteristics and climate, a central computer-based college guidance program sponsored by an organization such as the College Board would be able to direct each student's attention, as well as that of his parents and his school guidance counselor, to those colleges that appear to match in several principal and significant respects the student's college expectations and requirements. Although in one respect this system would appear to narrow the student's choice of colleges, it would intentionally narrow it only with respect to those colleges that "fit" the student. Actually, by calling the student's attention to colleges with which he may otherwise be unfamiliar but which fit his abilities, needs, and interests, it would in effect widen his initial choice of colleges. Moreover, by the questions it asks and the information it provides, such a system should reduce substantially the problem of the student who eventually drops out of a particular college because the reality of college life is quite unlike his expectations.

It should be noted, however, that this proposed college guidance program would not be a brave new world in which computers would assign students to colleges. On the contrary, together with volumes of supplementary information about college in general, and colleges in particular, this would be an important first step in a series of steps by which each individual would find the college that would give him the education best suited to him and each college would find the student body it could best serve.

Also, in the effort to increase our understanding of each student's potential for college, we may expect continuing efforts to measure better the cognitive and noncognitive domains, to identify intellectual abilities, in addition to the verbal and the quantitative, that relate to academic success, and to improve the measurement of the nonintellectual traits such as interest and motivation—and even that will-o'-the-wisp, creativity—that obviously influence individual performance but resist reliable and valid measurement. Several recent studies have indicated the potential value of the factual and verifiable information provided by a student about himself. These studies have suggested that we can probably make much better use of this material as a supplement to what more conventional measures are likely to indicate about the student's potential for college achievement. Not surprisingly, what an individual has done may reveal more about the strength of his interests, his motives, or even his creativeness, than his self-report of his likes and dislikes or his personal estimate of his disposition to choose certain hypothetical alternatives.

On the other hand, we probably should not expect that the measurement of personality as it has been perceived in the past is likely to show improvement. Indeed, there is reason to believe that personality testing as such will never overcome the rightful suspicion with which it is now regarded. Recent research has raised more skepticism about what such tests measure than it has resolved. Moreover, it is doubtful that it is possible to construct valid personality tests that cannot be faked and, much worse, that do not encourage faking and other socially undesirable behavior. However, there is an increasing body of research, some of it done at Education Testing Service, which suggests that the personal style of individuals in solving problems is a measurable individual trait that is related to success in certain kinds of tasks. These cognitive styles of individuals, such as the tendency of some to sharpen a conclusion while the tendency of others is to generalize it, or the tendency of some to classify phenomena, objects, or people into a few broad categories while the tendency of others is to use many separate categories, may well provide the basis for future tests which, together with other information, will help schools and colleges guide each student to the college curriculum that offers him the optimal opportunity for learning. Tests of cognitive style, by showing how certain problem-solving strategies are more effective for solving certain kinds of problems and by providing clues as to how to teach students to use different strategies for the solution of different problems, may also help educators to discover ways to improve individual learning.

But the changes in testing for college entrance may be less radical than the changes that the colleges may adopt for testing at the college level. As the colleges experiment with new approaches for fulfilling their responsibility to educate a greatly expanded and more diverse college population, testing should help colleges to increase their educational potential and institutional flexibility.

For example, some colleges may find a need for tests that give recognition and encouragement to independent study, both on campus and off. Some colleges will need tests to assess the achievement of large numbers of transfer students coming to them from two-year and four-year institutions. Those with new or expanded programs of continuing education will need a means of counseling and placing individuals whose education is the combined product of interrupted formal schooling, informal study, and work experience. Some colleges will introduce individual courses or entire courses of study that employ external examinations as a basis for demonstrating satisfactory completion.

Innovation and expansion are likely to encourage many colleges to make much wider use of standardized college-level tests of achievement than has traditionally been the case. We may expect to see the development of national and local testing programs that will provide tests for a wide variety of college subjects, including not only the typical academic ones but, as the definition of the college curriculum expands, professional and technical subjects as well. In addition, colleges will find existing and new tests of general education at the college level to be of increasing value for a whole variety of purposes ranging from curriculum evaluation to the screening of transfer students.

But perhaps the most interesting development may be the increasing use of tests by colleges to provide credit and placement for individuals whose academic careers do not fit the conventional pattern and by means of such tests to encourage unconventional patterns for those students who may profit educationally from such an approach. In order to make optimum use of their limited resources in a period when the demand for education will threaten to overwhelm the supply of competent faculty, colleges may encourage students capable of undertaking it to progress toward a degree by such means of independent study as those involving the new techniques of television, programmed learning, and computer-based instruction, or by the old-fashioned ones of reading, work, or travel, all of which would be validated and credited by means of tests. The tests, employing both multiple-choice and essay questions, would represent standards of achievement acceptable to college faculties. They would have been planned and developed by college teachers and validated against the performance of college students enrolled in regular college courses.

Tests somewhat similar to these have been used by the United States Armed Forces Institute for a number of years with moderate success in obtaining college credit for servicemen who pass the tests. Since 1960, a number of developments indicate an increasing college interest in such tests. The New York State College Proficiency Examinations Program demonstrated that liberal arts colleges are in principle willing to support the use of such tests for awarding college credit. The Committee on Institutional Cooperation (composed of representatives of the Big Ten and the University of Chicago) proposed the establishment of an interuniversity clearinghouse that would facilitate and stimulate credit-by-examination. And, most recently, the College Entrance Examination Board announced the establishment of a Council on College-Level Examinations that will within the next few years attempt the development of a national system of placement and credit-by-examination. Many colleges have for years given token recognition to the concept of credit-by-examination by making provision for it in their regulations. Some colleges do occasionally award credit-by-examination to a few students on the basis of locally developed tests. Few colleges do more. A "look forward in testing" suggests that in the future colleges will rely on externally developed tests administered nationally to provide credit and placement by examination for regularly enrolled students as well as for special students whose affiliation with the college does not conform to the conventional pattern. By doing so the colleges will have made an important adaptation to the individual differences in intellectual achievement, motivation, and growth among college students.

Further, it is not unlikely that, as some colleges look for additional ways to improve standards of excellence, they may look toward the appointment of boards of examiners similar to those that have worked effectively at the University of Chicago, Michigan State University, and on a few other campuses. Composed mainly of faculty members who have received some training in test development, each board of examiners would be able to provide course examinations, particularly for courses enrolling relatively large numbers of students, that reflect the unique objectives of its college's courses and are geared to its college's level of instruction and its students' abilities. Such boards of examiners would not be restricted to essay or multiple-choice tests but would be able to help the faculty make the best use of all types of examinations.

However, for many colleges the creation of their own boards of examiners will be difficult and expensive. Although nearly all college teachers test, few college teachers are trained in testing. And a relatively small college may not wish to devote to testing and evaluation a substantial amount of the time of a few members of its faculty. The alternative for those colleges interested in the ends to be served but unable to find the means to achieve them would be a college examinations service that could serve groups of colleges having relatively similar curricula. The college examinations service would have a large pool of questions that had been developed for college course examinations. With the cooperation of those colleges that have had boards of examiners and testing agencies such as Educational Testing Service, the college examinations service would be able to begin its activity with a substantial pool of questions. Each of the questions would be classified as to subject and skill measured, and, if the data are available, as to its difficulty for a defined student population. The questions would be stored in a computer. When a college requested a test for one of its courses, it would, on forms provided by the college examinations service, specify the course objectives to be measured (probably in terms of content, skills, and so on) and the weight that each objective should receive in the test. With this information, the computer would produce from its storehouse of questions a test matching the specifications provided by the college and including an alternate for each question in the test. The computer-assembled test would then be sent to the college for review by its faculty. In this review, the faculty could reject any question and choose its alternate, revise it, or write a substitute. After the test had been administered by the college, the results would be reported to the examinations service so that the data on student performance on each question could be stored in the computer to help subsequent users of the questions. Each college using the service would pay a fee to cover the maintenance of the service and the preparation of new questions for the computer bank. Colleges would be encouraged to construct additional questions for the bank by offering them a credit for each new question contributed. The college examinations service would also make available to the colleges technical consultation on test use and interpretation. If successful, a college examinations service would provide each participating college with the equivalent of its own board of examiners and the means to use the most sophisticated testing methods for the evaluation and improvement of instruction.

New ways for colleges to assess college-level achievement, while necessary and important, may not, however, be sufficient if colleges are to fulfill their responsibility to the individual student. A growing body of opinion, supported by research, maintains that colleges need to do much more to adapt the contents of their curricula and the climates of their campuses to the needs of changing student populations. In an earlier paper, Robert Pace has suggested the principle that the more education is sought by the masses, the less adequate are mass methods of education. I suggest that there is an analogy between the history of elementary and high school education in the last half-century and the situation in which the colleges will find themselves in the next half-century. As the elementary and then the high schools have been faced with the need to provide education for an increasing proportion of the population, they have been obliged to modify and supplement their curricula to accommodate the needs and interests of all their students—to make education inclusive rather than exclusive. The colleges are on the threshold of a period in which they may be faced by a similar obligation to adapt their educational programs to provide for the diversity of the new college student population. McConnell and Heist, in *The American College,* have suggested that "the efficacy of a college is the product of the fortunate conjunction of student characteristics and expectations, *and* the demands, sanctions, and opportunities of the college environment and its subcultures."[1] We know that colleges differ almost as much as students and that different types of students do best in different college environments. The challenge to the colleges is to adapt their environments to provide for these different needs of different students. To do so, colleges will need to gather new kinds of information about student characteristics and expectations and the demands, sanctions, and opportunities of the college environment and its subcultures, and to study the interrelationships between such factors and students' intellectual and personal growth.

This will require relatively new types of instruments. One such is Robert Pace's *College & University Environment Scales* (CUES).[2]

---

[1] T. R. McConnell and Paul Heist, "The Diverse College Student Population," in Nevitt Sanford, ed., *The American College* (New York: John Wiley & Sons, Inc., 1962), p. 250.

[2] C. Robert Pace, *College & University Environment Scales* (Princeton, New Jersey: Educational Testing Service, 1962).

CUES is not a measure of the individual student but of the institution which he attends. It is designed to describe the intellectual-social-cultural climate of the campus along five dimensions: the degree to which personal status and practical benefit are emphasized in the college environment; the degree to which the campus is friendly, cohesive, and group-oriented; the degree of emphasis on self-understanding and personal identity, a wide range of appreciations, and personal involvement with the problems of the world; the degree to which politeness, protocol, and consideration are emphasized; and the degree to which competitively high academic achievement is evidenced with concern for scholarship and intellectual discipline and interest in knowledge and ideas.

Another type of instrument are the College Student Questionnaires (CSQ)[3] developed by Educational Testing Service to facilitate the study of biographical and attitudinal characteristics of groups of college students at different stages of their college careers. Part I of CSQ is designed for administration to entering students at the beginning of the academic year and contains questions about educational and vocational plans and expectations; activities, achievements, and perceptions during high school; family background; and certain attitudes and values. Part II of CSQ is administered to undergraduates toward the end of the academic year. It repeats questions concerning educational and vocational plans and attitudes and values, and thus enables colleges to study student change. In addition, it contains questions dealing with students' perceptions, satisfactions, and activities as students at the college.

Instruments such as CUES and CSQ, used together with tests of aptitude and achievement, provide the colleges with the institutional research tools needed to take the initial step toward adapting the college to the individual student. The implications for creating improved environments for learning are exciting. For a long time we have ranked colleges as "good" or "poor" on the basis of the quality of their graduates, knowing full well that in a great many cases the "good" colleges produced good students because they admitted good students. However, we need to know more about the colleges that nurture the greatest intellectual and personal growth in their students and to know which are the key factors in those colleges that contribute to students' growth. This is, perhaps, the most significant way in which tests can help the college fulfill its responsibility to the individual student. A "look forward in testing" underscores the exciting promise of a forward look in higher education.

[3] *College Student Questionnaires* (Princeton, New Jersey: Educational Testing Service, 1965).

W. Max Wise

COUNSELING INDIVIDUALS IN
LIBERAL ARTS COLLEGES

ONE OF THE REMARKABLE DEVELOPMENTS IN AMERICAN HIGHER EDUCA-
tion during the past twenty years has been the rapid growth of counseling
activities and the acceptance of these activities as an essential part of our
collegiate institutions. Few presidents of our colleges feel that they can
ignore the need for such services and many cite the provision of professional counseling services as evidence of strength in their institutions.

Yet, my observations lead me to believe that many college presidents
feel they have limited perspective with respect to these developments and
are therefore unable to provide strong leadership for policy decisions about
the forms of counseling services appropriate to their individual campuses
and the commitment of college funds to such functions. My remarks
are intended to describe some of these developments in broad outline
and to indicate the importance of recent emphases which, I believe,
may affect both the perspectives with which we view counseling of college students and the forms which these activities will assume in liberal
arts colleges.

It is now more than seventy-five years since the first "student deans"
were appointed in American colleges. These early positions were
established to perpetuate the traditional parietal functions of the American colleges but were also aimed at meeting the challenges imposed
by the liberalization of the American undergraduate curriculum and
the decline of the rigid authoritarianism of our early colleges in the
supervision of student social life.

As early as the first decade in the ninetenth century the harsh, parental authority of the American college had been modified, partly because
of student reaction but also because new educational ideas were intro-

duced which challenged the bases on which our early colleges were founded. In our first colleges little initiative was left to the student. His day was supervised and he was assumed to be a ward of the college—being an adolescent at the time of admission (about age fourteen) this assumption seemed well founded. His academic program, too, was closely supervised and consisted mainly of instruction from textbooks and disputations led by the staff of the college.

By the late nineteenth century the educational purposes of our earliest colleges had ceased to reflect an almost exclusive interest in education for citizenship and moral training. The colleges had begun to incorporate background training for careers as physicians, lawyers, engineers, and the like. While moral training continued to be taken for granted, a loosening of the curriculum elevated certain intellectual virtues which assumed a parallel, if not a dominant, importance in the liberal arts colleges. Descriptive scholarship, as opposed to proscriptive scholarship, grew in importance, especially as the scientific studies were accepted into the liberal arts curriculum.

Perhaps the most powerful influences which eroded the restrictive nature of early college life resulted from the transformation of the national social life to incorporate pluralism and the rise of a pragmatic view of the nature of human affairs and human problems.

The early student deans were expected to form relationships with students which would effect a substitution of moral influence for the restrictive and oppressive regimentation which had been challenged by the changes in the social and intellectual life of the nation. The hope was that the moral influence of the student deans might be accomplished in a friendly manner but if that failed coercive means were used.

The rise in the number of course offerings and a loosening of the curriculum to include electives were additional factors which prompted many colleges to appoint student deans as counselors.

The strains on the old social order in our colleges and the first stirrings of important work in social sciences led a few leaders, by the turn of the century, to urge that student counseling should be based on a more scientific study of the students. As early as the first decade of this century, President William Rainey Harper of the University of Chicago predicted that the scientific study of college students would provide a more rational and effective basis for counseling.

But the scientific approach to counseling college students had to wait until the development of measurement instruments during the First World War. Following the development of tests designed to place draftees in the most appropriate assignments in the Army, Ben D. Wood of Columbia, W. H. Cowley and Donfred H. Gardner of Ohio, and others, proposed that such tests should be used for the classification of college students and that they would be particularly helpful in rendering decisions with respect to applicants for admission to colleges. They also proposed that the results of measurement would be helpful in counseling students with respect to the choice of major fields and with respect to vocational planning. By 1926, American colleges were experimenting with the use of measurement devices for such purposes and the remarkable growth of the use of tests since that time is too well known to require documentation here.

A new basis for counseling students in the liberal arts colleges was developed and, following the lead of the Army and of industry, came to be known as "personnel" work. Through this period the new psychometrically oriented counselors were added to the colleges but the older versions of counseling, representing the wish of the college to affect the moral influence, also remained. Thus, it was common in the late twenties and early thirties for liberal arts colleges to employ trained psychologists to administer psychometric devices and to discuss the results with students, but it was also common for the colleges to appoint deans of men and deans of women to act as counselors.

The fact that the measurement instruments were primarily designed to classify large groups of persons into subgroups with discriminate abilities and aptitudes did not deter enthusiasts who looked to the use of measurement results as a firm basis for counseling individuals. The warnings of several prominent American educators, John Dewey among them, that the indiscriminate use of measurement results would have a negative effect on American education were largely ignored. In a book published in 1927,[1] Kelley noted that a reliability coefficient of .50 was sufficient to distinguish two class-sized groups, at a modest level of confidence, but that a reliability coefficient of .94 would be required to distinguish a score made by an individual student from scores made by other students with the same degree of confidence. The level of confidence used by Kelley, a probability of 5 to 1 that the score actually discriminated, was an arbitrary one but the principle applied to any level of confidence chosen. Kelley concluded that the reliability coefficients of the measurement instruments available in 1927 were such as to cast doubt on their usefulness in discriminating the abilities and aptitudes of individual students.

Such cautions were largely ignored by educators in their enthusiasm to incorporate measurement results into counseling activities. Even at this date, few counselors are aware of the limitations which logic forces on the use of test data in counseling and there is little discussion of these matters in the literature. A recent and thoughtful exploration by

[1] Truman Lee Kelley, *Interpretation of Educational Measurements* (Yonkers, New York: Harcourt, Brace & World, Inc., 1927).

Cronbach and Gleser, for instance, is largely unknown, yet the conclusions they reached appear extremely relevant:

> In the literature on counseling, one finds numerous references to the responsibility of the counselor for helping the client make the right decision. The "right decision" is almost invariably interpreted as being that course of action in which his mean expectancy of success is greatest. This viewpoint has two faults. One is the implicit assumption that one particular decision is best for all persons having the same pattern of test scores. Our discussion of individual evaluations implies that two students might draw different conclusions from the same data and both be correct. Secondly, the assumption that the mean of the distribution of outcomes is the proper index must be questioned.[2]

A major, but inadvertent, result of the indiscriminate use of test data in counseling college students has been to reinforce the feeling of such students that the college is not interested in their individuality.

Two major effects of the use of measurement techniques in counseling college students may be observed:

1.   Discussions between college students and their counselors, once concerned with the individual student's moral and ethical responses to the rules of the college and to the society, have been transformed to more dispassionate and objective conversations. Much use has been made of information concerning the abilities and aptitudes of the college students as revealed through the use of measurement devices, and test data have been widely accepted as an important basis for decision making. Thus, development of measurement instruments has helped transfer counseling to a logical basis more consistent with the new values in American intellectual life.

2.   In our enthusiasm to transfer the counseling of college students to a scientific basis little attention has been paid to the cautions which should be observed in the application of measurement techniques. Warnings that the indiscriminate use of measurement data would have the effect of reducing the freedom of individuals were issued during the 1920's, but these admonitions have been largely ignored.

In summary, the widespread use of measurement data in student counseling provided a means of transforming work with students from essentially moralistic bases to more objective ones. Thus, the new developments served a very important function but they also set a stage for the reaction which had developed by the time of the beginning of the Second World War.

After the first enthusiasm for the use of measurement devices in

---

[2] Lee J. Cronbach and Goldine C. Gleser, *Psychological Tests and Personnel Decisions* (Urbana: University of Illinois Press, 1957), p. 117.

college counseling had subsided, many counselors began the search for an intellectual basis on which to develop a revival of the affective component of student counseling. It was apparent to such people that the use of measurement devices alone provided a severely restricted basis for conversations with students. They saw too many examples of students whose indicated aptitudes for college work, as revealed by test data, were at wide variance with their actual performance in our collegiate institutions. By the mid-thirties the search for ideas had turned to the field of psychotherapy and by the end of the Second World War college counselors were making wide use of psychiatric concepts.

The field of psychotherapy provided two needed correctives to the previous emphases in college counseling:

1.   It reaffirmed the importance of individual reactions as a factor in helping college students make productive use of the opportunity for higher education. The clarification of perceptions of the self and the social world in which the individual lived was taken for granted by those working in the field of psychiatry and these concepts were widely adopted by college counselors. The publication of *Counseling and Psychotherapy* by Carl R. Rogers, in 1942, was widely applauded in American higher education and by the close of the Second World War the concept of "client-centered" counseling had assumed considerable importance among those engaged in college counseling.

2.   In general, the logic of psychotherapy emphasized that the responses of young adults were substantially the result of early childhood experiences in the family and in the school, that such response patterns were unconsciously followed by individuals, and that they were only slightly modifiable. Thus, the college student was portrayed as constrained by early influences in his life of which he was largely unaware and psychotherapists engaged students in conversations which were intended to make these early influences conscious in the life of the individual. In the main, psychotherapists hoped to clarify these unconscious influences and help the student "adjust" to them.

Both of the major developments mentioned above contributed to the professional development of counseling in American liberal arts colleges. Coupled with the Federal programs for counseling returned veterans in the postwar colleges, these two developments led to the establishment of special counseling services in most of our institutions of higher education. One of the most remarkable developments in the history of higher education in this country is the rapid growth of such professional services during the decade from 1946 through 1956. These centers of professional services have contributed significantly to the alleviation of individual distress among American college students and have freed many students for productive academic work. They therefore deserve widespread support by educational administrators and have in general received such support.

The development of professional counseling has, however, had remarkably little effect on the individual professor's understanding of the students with whom he works and may even have reduced the responsibility which he is willing to assume for thoughtful, informal conversations with his students, since many professors assume that such conversations are the responsibility of professional counselors. Nevertheless, the efficacy of professional counseling based on the careful application of measurement theory and on concepts derived from psychotherapy has been so well demonstrated that few American liberal arts colleges have dared to ignore these developments.

The most important recent development which has influenced counseling in the liberal arts colleges arises from the revived interests of sociologists and the new interest of anthropologists in the study of American college students and the institutions in which they enroll. It is interesting to note that there was considerable interest among American sociologists in such studies during the late twenties and early thirties but that this interest declined sharply by 1935. Only in the last ten years have sociologists revived their earlier interests. The interest of anthropologists in such studies is very new. One commentator has suggested that since anthropologists have exhausted primitive societies as a focus of field work they have been forced to turn their attention to the American society.

Both groups of American scholars—sociologists and anthropologists—have recently undertaken the description of the social context within which students and faculty work. The result has been to provide contextual views of the individual student in his interactions with his fellow students and the faculty as well as in his interaction with the organizational structure of the college.

The pioneering work of Theodore M. Newcomb at Bennington College in the late thirties and the more recent work of Nevitt Sanford and his associates at Vassar have suggested the importance of peer groups and institutional press as factors which influence the reactions of students to their colleges and to the purposes of liberal education.

It seems fair to say that until very recently the sociological and anthropological studies have continued to focus on the psychological and sociological processes through which the students move with little or no attention paid to the intellectual processes which are characteristic of American undergraduate liberal arts studies. While the studies referred to above have been extremely helpful in providing insight into the nature of the social world in which American students live, little attention has been paid to the effects of the intellectual experience through which most students move.

There is some tentative evidence which suggests that the responses of individual students to their colleges are affected by the intellectual content of the curriculum. While few definitive studies have been completed at this time, several are under way and the results will be available soon.

In a study which is nearing completion, William Perry, Director of the Harvard Bureau of Study Counsel, has investigated the importance of the intellectual component of undergraduate liberal arts education. Using data collected from several classes of Harvard undergraduates, Perry has hypothesized that most students move through three stages of reaction to the intellectual life of the institution:

1. At the beginning of their collegiate experience, a sizable number of undergraduates have a dualistic view of the intellectual realm. Having been trained to solve problems by finding "correct" answers they view most of the intellectual undertaking as consisting of determining right and wrong answers. The problem for the student is to use logic or authority to buttress the argument for the right answer.

2. One of the effects of the first year or two of undergraduate liberal arts study, Perry notes, is that the student learns that most of the important questions under study have no right or wrong answers and he concludes therefore that a high degree of relativism is involved. The immediate result is to force the student into a new intellectual mood which challenges most of the ethical and moral concepts he formerly held. He is no longer able to use simple logic or to quote authority in order to find the right answer but must face the prospect that there is no right answer at all. He begins to understand that in solving substantial questions the suppositions with which one begins and the context within which the problem is considered have much to do with the nature of the answer. The result often is that the student undergoes a psychological reaction which undermines his previously held moral and ethical concepts and which produces the first crisis in his response to the college. There is some evidence that the grasp of relativistic views of the intellectual life calls his own identity into question also.

3. The successful undergraduate liberal arts student progresses beyond simple relativism to a point where he is willing to accept ambiguity and he moves to a stage which Perry is prepared to call commitment. In this stage, the student perceives that most important questions have a relativistic component and that what is required for productive intellectual functioning is to accept the fact that answers are never final but, based on the evidence available, one must accept the answer best suited to the situation which one faces.

Perry has documented the fact that drastic changes have occurred in the modes of teaching at Harvard between 1900 and 1960 and all these changes have emphasized the relativistic nature of human knowledge.

Several other studies in process are designed to explore the contextual relationships within which the liberal arts college students live. These studies show promise of helping those interested in counseling individual students to deal more perceptively with the student as he encounters the thrust of the modern American college.

Obviously, if such contextual studies are successful, there may well be a revival of the interest of faculty members in counseling students. The new concepts are closely related to the intellectual life of the college and to the curriculum and there is little reason for faculty members to continue to believe that the professional psychologists and psychiatrists should carry the full responsibility for counseling.

These recent developments suggest the possibility that counseling of individual college students will soon be restored to a more central position on the college campus. It seems possible that such developments will restore the balance which is badly needed in American higher education between the professional counselors on the one hand and members of the faculty on the other.

JB Lon Hefferlin

RECENT RESEARCH ON COLLEGE STUDENTS

In our new study of institutional vitality in American colleges and universities, we at the Institute of Higher Education are building our research on the work of other scholars of higher education elsewhere in the country who have been studying the impact of college on students.

In this presentation, let me report several findings from these other studies of the impact of college on students and then alert you to three particularly interesting studies of students and their colleges that will be published in the next year or two. Of the research on students during the past decade, the most significant for college administrators, professors, and student personnel officers has been, to my mind, that concerned with student culture and student peer groups. Because of these studies we now know a good deal about the important role that students themselves play on most campuses in setting standards for each other's achievement and accomplishment. The studies that I want to report here lead me to conclude that if college officials do not sense the attitudes and orientation of the student groups on their campuses and fail to base their educational practices on this information, their institutions will continue to remain less than effective from their point of view.

My theme can be summarized in two quotations. The first is from James S. Coles, President of Bowdoin College, who has stated that "it is not reasonable to expect that what the best professors can do in fifteen hours in the classroom can be fully effective if the remaining hours of the student's week are spent in an environment unsympathetic to what the professor would accomplish."[1] And the second is from Nevitt San-

---

[1] James S. Coles, "Introductory Remarks," *Proceedings of the Symposium on Undergraduate Environment, October 18–19, 1962* (Brunswick, Me.: Bowdoin College, 1963), p. 7.

ford, who says, "I would put it down as a general rule that students cannot go against the value systems of their peers unless there are rewarding attachments to adults—and with an accompanying intellectual understanding which shows the superiority of the adult system."[2]

Let me point to some recent findings that support these opinions. Consider first the perennial problem of cheating. A young sociologist at Columbia University, William J. Bowers, became interested in this problem as an undergraduate at Washington and Lee, where he noticed that some of his fellow students who had cheated in high school were apparently not continuing to cheat in college. Bowers was curious about whether the negative attitude of the other Washington and Lee students toward cheating might account for this change, and when he came to Columbia's Bureau of Applied Social Research he undertook a comparative study of student dishonesty in American colleges. He found that at some of the ninety-nine participating colleges as few as 4 per cent of the students he questioned admitted that they had cheated, while at other institutions up to 89 per cent of the students reported doing so. Looking at the correlates of low levels of cheating, he discovered that the norms and values held by the other students at the college, and particularly by a student's immediate peer group, have a stronger, more powerful effect on discouraging cheating than any other factors he measured. The influence of these norms and values was more pronounced, for example, than the student's own prior attitude toward cheating or his success or lack of success in obtaining good grades.

This climate of peer disapproval of cheating is particularly important, as you can imagine, in colleges with student honor codes. These honor codes seem to institutionalize the disapproving attitude of the students. Thus Bowers reports,

> The level of cheating is much lower at schools that place primary responsibility for dealing with cases of academic dishonesty in the hands of students and their elected representatives, as under the honor system, than at schools that rely on faculty-centered control or have a form of mixed control, in which faculty and students jointly participate.[3]

One particular example of the importance of the attitudes of peers came to light in the 1964 investigation of the cheating incident at the Air Force Academy. A Special Advisory Committee, with General Thomas D. White as its chairman, was formed to carry out the investigation and make recommendations to the Secretary and Chief of Staff of

[2] Nevitt Sanford, "General Education and the Theory of Personality Development," *ibid.,* p. 10.

[3] William J. Bowers, *Student Dishonesty and Its Control in College* (New York: Bureau of Applied Social Research, Columbia University, December 1964), p. 198.

the Air Force. The Committee found that cheating was not randomly distributed within the Academy. Instead, "the cheating tended to concentrate in squadrons where, the Committee was informed, cadets regarded their AOC's [Air Officers Commanding] as uncommunicative, preoccupied with standardization, or overly concerned with petty detail." A number of cadets who cheated "came to the distorted view," in the opinion of the Committee, "that their primary loyalties were to each other, rather than to the Wing."[4]

The impact of such peer pressures, for good or ill, is not confined to undergraduates and to undergraduate colleges: It exists equally in professional schools, as witness the study of first-year medical school students by Blanche Geer, Everett Hughes, and Howard Becker, entitled *Boys in White*,[5] or Charles D. Orth's study of first-year students at the Harvard Graduate School of Business Administration. As a faculty member in the Graduate School of Business Administration, Orth was aware that many of his fellow faculty members, like many professors elsewhere, assume that the extent of their students' learning is predominantly determined by their teaching ability, the content of their courses, and the institution's rules and regulations. But from his earlier experience as a student in the school, Orth wondered if it was possible that "the academic performance of our students is influenced as much or more by their need for social acceptance [by their peers] as by the rewards offered by the Faculty."[6] He examined the social system which developed among the students during the first year of the business school program and found that most students got signals from their peers that "maximum achievement was a social crime."[7] "Many students," he concluded, "feel that rewards from their peers are at least as valuable as those offered by the Faculty. They therefore limit their class performance to a point between the minimum acceptable level set by the Faculty and the maximum acceptable level set by their peers."[8]

Across the Charles River from Harvard's business school, the staff members of the Harvard Student Study are finding that the influence of peers within the Harvard Houses seems to be the predominant pressure in changing some of the values and attitudes of Harvard undergraduates over the three years they are in the Houses. Rebecca Vreeland

[4] *Report to the Secretary and Chief of Staff of the Air Force by the Special Advisory Committee on the United States Air Force Academy 5 May 1965* (Washington, D.C.: Department of the Air Force, 1965), pp. 43, 62.

[5] Howard S. Becker *et al., Boys in White* (Chicago: University of Chicago Press, 1961).

[6] Charles D. Orth, III, *Social Structure and Learning Climate; The First Year at the Harvard Business School* (Boston: Division of Research, Graduate School of Business Administration, Harvard University, 1963), p. 18.

[7] *Ibid.,* p. 213.

[8] *Ibid.,* p. 220.

and Charles Bidwell, the two staff members examining the social structure of the college, have identified "peer involvement in the House" as a primary mechanism "for the transmission of House goals and student norms, and thus as a source of attitude and value change. Although other mechanisms may be at work, when peer involvement is high, House effects upon student value and attitude change are marked."[9]

In comparing the impact of student values to that of faculty values, the impressions of students themselves have been studied with somewhat similar results. For example, E. K. Wilson has analyzed the autobiographical statements of a sample of Antioch College students in terms of the changes that they felt they had undergone in college. Seven different changes were most frequently mentioned by the students, and Theodore Newcomb reports Wilson's results as follows:

> Most of these kinds of changes were thought to be influenced both by teachers and by fellow students, but with some provocative differences. The only kinds of changes attributed more frequently to teachers than to students were those labeled "intellectual" and "career plans and choices." Four of the remaining five were attributed at least twice as frequently to peers as to teachers: "interest in new fields," "personality development," "social development," and "attitude toward Antioch College." . . . From such data I conclude, again, that courses and teachers are necessary but not sufficient inducers of change: peer influence is also essential.[10]

Similar results have been reported at Michigan State, where Irvin J. Lehmann and Paul L. Dressel report that their analysis of student interviews and questionnaires "strongly suggested that discussions and 'bull-sessions' were a potent factor in shaping the attitudes and values of these college students. . . . Instructors and/or courses were infrequently mentioned by these students as having had some impact upon their behavior or perspective in life."[11]

In sum, there is now good evidence for the belief, long held by some educators, that the dominant influences on most American college students are not their professors, not their courses, not their books and lecturers—but their fellow students. This conclusion may

[9] Rebecca Vreeland and Charles Bidwell, "Organizational Effects on Student Attitudes: A Study of the Harvard Houses," *Sociology of Education,* 38:3 (Spring 1965), p. 247.

[10] Theodore M. Newcomb, "Research on Student Characteristics: Current Approaches," in *The Student in Higher Education* (Background Papers for Participants in the 1965 Annual Meeting, American Council on Education; Washington, D.C.: American Council on Education, 1965), p. 57.

[11] Irvin J. Lehmann and Paul L. Dressel, *Critical Thinking, Attitudes, and Values in Higher Education* (East Lansing: Michigan State University, 1962), p. 268.

have been obvious to all of you, but I know that some professors and administrators continue to fight losing educational battles because they neglect its implications. At their institutions, if the gulf between the curriculum and the extracurriculum is ever to be bridged, if student life and student learning are ever to be integrated, and if enthusiastic emotion and calm reason in the life of the students are some day to benefit each other, professors and administrators must concern themselves with the total impact of the campus on students and work for its improvement beyond the classroom.

Moreover, to narrow the gap between the peer culture of the students and the academic culture of the professoriate, the efforts of faculty members and administrators at most colleges must be based on another finding of studies of students: a finding that the attitudes of students toward their own role as students, toward their college, and toward their aims in college are molded and set early in their college days.

Several studies have demonstrated this significance of the freshman year for attitude change. For example, Lehmann and Dressel found at Michigan State that students' value orientations and their ability in critical thinking changed most during the freshman year, and that after the junior year, many students reached a plateau with respect to their value orientations. And a recent study of a well-known midwestern liberal arts college by Walter Wallace indicates that at least some major attitude changes occur primarily within the first few months of college. Wallace, then at the National Opinion Research Center and now at Northwestern University, took measures of the students' academic and social orientations to college life at three points during their first year: once during orientation week, again in November, and again in May. Peter Rossi, the director of the National Opinion Research Center, has summarized Wallace's findings in this way:

> . . . It was immediately obvious that massive changes had taken place during this relatively brief period. Students coming into the school placed high valuation on academic achievement, but toward the end of the freshman year had lowered their levels of aspiration concerning grades and the importance of grades to that of the rest of the school. Indeed, the major shift in value emphasis occurred during the period between September and November indicating that socialization to the normative system of the school occurred in a short period of time and involved changes of considerable magnitude.[12]

Rossi indicates that two similar studies, one at the University of Chicago and another among army units, uncovered similar results.

[12] Peter I. Rossi, unpublished work paper, Research Conference on Social Science Methods and Student Residences, Ann Arbor, University of Michigan, November 28–29, 1964, p. 3.

All three studies indicated that massive socialization effects occurred during the initial few weeks of entry into the institutions in question, that effects were greatest among those individuals who were most oriented toward their peers, and that changes beyond the early weeks were relatively slight, as long as the individual remained in the institution in question.[13]

Rossi has hence made these three suggestions to college administrators who desire to bring to bear on students countervailing influences beyond those of their peers:

1. Strategies aimed at the first few weeks of entry experiences on the part of recruits [i.e., freshmen] are strategies which have the best chance of succeeding.

2. Barriers to communication between upper classmen and freshmen would aid in the development of a class by class subculture which would show some signs of changing an institution.

3. Devices to reduce the status gap between freshmen and upper classmen would aid in reducing upper class influence on entering freshmen, e.g., the creation of special groups of particularly high prestige within the freshman class.[14]

In short, if administrators and professors hope to avoid the usual covert warfare that pitches students against the staff in many American colleges, and hope to try to create instead the community of students and scholars that they desire, they might well concentrate on improving the opening encounters between professors and freshmen and also those between freshmen and returning students.

Additional studies on college students will be out soon: Three of particular interest will be those on undergraduate life at the University of Kansas by Blanche Geer and Howard Becker; on students at Bennington College and the University of Michigan by Theodore M. Newcomb and E. K. Wilson; and on six private liberal arts colleges and two public institutions by members of the staff of the Center for the Study of Higher Education at the University of California, Berkeley. They promise to provide us with additional insights on students, their reaction to college, and the impact of college on them.

[13] *Ibid.,* p. 4.
[14] *Ibid.,* p. 5.

David E. Fox

PRESENTATION OF ATTRITION STUDY

ALTHOUGH THIS IS AN AGE IN WHICH COLLEGE ENROLLMENTS ARE escalating and higher education is making significant strides toward more effective educational techniques and better facilities, the rate of student attrition is the same today as it has been over the past forty years. Two national studies of attrition, one by McNeeley in 1937[1] and the other by Iffert in 1957,[2] revealed that only 40 per cent of all students entering college receive their degrees after four years of undergraduate study while another 20 per cent graduate at a later time. Thus, 40 per cent of those who enter higher education do not complete their undergraduate education. One-third of these drop out due to academic failure, but the majority of students who leave college do so voluntarily. Attrition presents serious problems to the college in terms of underconsumed services and to the nation in terms of wasted human resources. The student who leaves college before he completes his course of studies sometimes suffers severely from the frustration of his ambitions.

John Summerskill, writing in *The American College*, gives three reasons why colleges and college presidents are concerned about attrition. The first is based on the concept that the college is organized as a "training center" rather than as an "intellectual center." "Colleges are supposed to qualify young people for entrance to careers. . . . In this tradition, when students fail to make the grade, disappointment and

---

[1] John H. McNeeley, *College Student Mortality,* United States Office of Education Bulletin, 1937, No. 11 (Washington, D.C.: Government Printing Office, 1938).

[2] Robert E. Iffert, *Retention and Withdrawal of College Students,* United States Office of Education Bulletin, 1958, No. 1 (Washington, D.C.: Government Printing Office, 1957).

hostility are frequently directed at the college, and the college with a high attrition rate is criticized for doing a poor job—regardless of the quality of its teaching and research."[3] Second, as the institutions expand and operating costs and faculty salaries increase, efficiency becomes a concern of the administrator. "The nature and extent of student losses constitute one measure of the efficiency of any educational institution."[4] A third reason for the study of attrition arises from the fact that ". . . dollars leave the income side of the budget when students leave the college. . . . When student attrition is high the college budget, typically under strain, may be unable to meet expenses. . . ."[5] In addition to the three reasons described by Summerskill, a fourth source of concern about attrition is our democratic society's need for educated manpower and educated citizens. Every student who withdraws from our colleges and universities reduces the reserve of educated manpower.

The administrative, economic, and social concerns connected with student attrition have resulted in much research. This research can be divided roughly into four categories: analytical, descriptive, census, and evaluative.

Analytical studies, as defined by the 1964 Research Conference on College Dropouts held at the University of Tennessee, are those ". . . concerned with reviewing characteristics of students, dropout trends, time of dropout and a host of possible cause and effect variables."[6]

Descriptive studies include those designed to identify the students' values and changes in values, their opinions of college courses and faculty, and the institutions' influences on the students. Such studies have investigated type of college, size of high school graduating class, and age of entering students as factors affecting attrition. The students' reasons for withdrawing have been tabulated from official college records, exit interviews, and questionnaires. Many studies of this type have explored the correlation between persistence in college and high school grades, aptitude and placement test scores, parents' financial status, and many other variables.

Evaluative studies are those designed to test specific programs. Generally they use control and experimental groups to measure changes that occur in the college environment when variables are altered. Most

---

[3] John Summerskill, "Dropouts from College," in Nevitt Sanford, ed., *The American College* (New York: John Wiley and Sons, Inc., 1962), p. 628.

[4] *Ibid.*, p. 628, citing F. I. Sheeder, "Student Losses in a Liberal Arts College," *Journal of American Association of College Registrars,* 15, 1939, pp. 34–40.

[5] Summerskill, *op. cit.,* pp. 628–629.

[6] James R. Montgomery, Project Director, *Proceedings of the Research Conference on College Dropouts,* U.S. Cooperative Research Project Number F-065 (Knoxville, Tennessee: The University of Tennessee, 1965), p. 48.

of the recommendations for future study suggested at the Tennessee Conference fell into the category of evaluative research.

The two best-known studies of attrition, those by McNeeley and Iffert, are of the census type. Both investigations were carried out by the United States Office of Education and were national in scope. The McNeeley sample included over nine thousand students who withdrew from twenty-four institutions between 1930–31 and 1934–35. Although some of McNeeley's results were substantiated by later studies, his findings were based on data from college records and one might question the efficacy of such records in revealing the students' reasons for withdrawal. Experience indicates that sufficiently extensive student personnel records are not maintained in most colleges even today. The McNeeley research, however, made educators more aware of the loss occurring through student attrition and paved the way for Iffert's study.

In 1957 Iffert completed a study of attrition based on an investigation of over twelve thousand students who entered 149 institutions of higher learning in 1950. He found, as did McNeeley, that the colleges lost approximately half of their students during the succeeding four years and graduated 39.5 per cent at the end of four years. He also determined that a maximum of 59 per cent of the entering students eventually graduated, and that there was a higher attrition rate in public than in private colleges.

In designing the study described in this report many previous studies were consulted, but Summerskill's analysis of earlier research on attrition provides a backdrop for the present review. Summerskill assembled and reviewed studies dating back forty years and arrived at the following generalizations concerning student withdrawal:[7]

1. Age at matriculation "does not affect attrition although older undergraduates may encounter more obstacles to graduation."
2. There is no significant difference between the attrition rate for men and that for women, but women tend to withdraw for different reasons than men.
3. Research findings are equivocal regarding the hypothesis that a student's economic and social background affects his adjustment to the environment of a college and is a factor in attrition. The influence of a particular student's socioeconomic background on his adjustment varies from one college to the next and is not in itself a reliable indicator of persistence in college.
4. Although size and location of the home are not particularly pertinent to withdrawal patterns, they do have a decided effect when they represent educational and cultural advantages and disadvantages which are different from those prevailing among the students at a given institution.

[7] Summerskill, *op. cit.*, pp. 631–647.

5. Several academic factors, including secondary school preparation, affect attrition. High school grades are probably the best indicator of success in college and are significantly related to attrition, but their value varies somewhat with the size and quality of the high school. Some evidence indicates "that students from larger high schools have significantly better chances of graduating from college."

Another reliable indicator of persistence in college appears to be scholastic aptitude tests. Research has shown that college dropouts have lower scholastic aptitude scores than the students who graduate, though the difference is not always a significant one.

Studies on the relationship of college grades to attrition indicate that approximately one student out of three leaves college because of academic failure. These figures are not to be taken at face value, because other research shows that "academic failure" often hides the student's inability to meet psychological, parental, social, or financial demands of college life. At the same time, true "academic failure" exists and reflects institutional failure in terms of "inadequate admissions procedures or inadequate instruction" as well as student shortcomings.

6. Motivation as a factor in attrition is difficult to measure because it is difficult to determine for which dropouts motivation is of primary importance. Most dropouts give two or more primary reasons for leaving as well as two additional contributing reasons. An often cited reason for withdrawal is lack of motivation, but it is not clear which motivational forces actually predict college success, nor is it known how to accurately measure such forces in students.

In general, students with definite vocational goals are more likely to succeed in college, but the characteristics and values of the institution selected also deserve consideration. For example, a vocationally motivated student who attends an institution which does not support strictly vocational goals may have considerable difficulty in adjusting.

7. If students' reasons for withdrawal are accepted at face value, failure to adjust to the campus environment causes a fairly low percentage of withdrawals. However, clinicians believe that students often conceal emotional maladjustment within the ostensibly more acceptable reasons which they offer at the time of withdrawal. But it is difficult to prove that signs of emotional maladjustment evident in some dropouts are not also evident in students who complete college.

8. Those who drop out due to illness, either of self or family, account for a small but significant portion of college dropouts. However, as a group, dropouts do not have substantially more illness than those students who persist to graduation.

9. Problems of personal finance ranked among the top three reasons for withdrawal. This determination is complicated by certain variables such as costs of attendance, the amount of scholarship aid given, the amount of part-time work done by students, and the constantly changing loan programs sponsored by the Federal government and certain states, as well as by private loan sources.

The many problems connected with student attrition are so broad that any one study can only scratch the surface. The greatest need is for comprehensive studies of attrition in individual institutions. The present study analyzes reasons for voluntary withdrawal in a group of private liberal arts colleges by examining the students' stated reasons for withdrawal and their reactions to college services and facilities. In tabulating results there was no effort to determine the extent to which reasons for withdrawal and other reactions were rationalizations of socially or personally less acceptable reasons. It is hoped the present effort will prove helpful in the review, evaluation, and improvement of college programs.

THE COLLEGES STUDIED

The twenty-one institutions which participated in the study are established, reputable, fully accredited, independent liberal arts colleges offering bachelor's degrees. Twenty of the colleges are church-related and one is not, while two are women's colleges and the remainder are coeducational. In full-time enrollment the colleges range from 501 to 1,368 students.

To provide a framework for further analysis, the participating colleges provided enrollment and attrition data in standardized form. Part of the data was compiled to show the percentage of withdrawals over a three-year period of those students classified as freshmen in 1960 and as seniors in the fall of 1963. The same procedure was used for the freshman class of 1961 which became the senior class in the fall of 1964. Additional data to determine the gross attrition rate were compiled for the total enrollment of each college for the one-year period from fall term 1963 to fall 1964. For all computations, students in the following categories were either excluded from institutional reports or considered withdrawals, as seemed appropriate:

1.   Those who went abroad in a planned, college-approved program during their junior year.
2.   Those who transferred to an affiliated college under the three-two plan.
3.   Those who entered after the first, or fall, registration period.
4.   Those who took additional or fewer courses than normal and, consequently, changed class status during the three years.

Table 1 contains the retention and withdrawal rates for seventeen of the twenty-one colleges. In many studies the withdrawal rate has been defined as the percentage of previously enrolled students who fail to graduate. However, since Iffert found that the senior year withdrawal

TABLE 1. College Retention and Withdrawal Rates for Full-time Students Classified as Freshmen in the Fall Terms of 1960 and 1961

| | Percentages of retention | | | | | | Percentages of withdrawal | | | | | |
| Insti- | MALE | | FEMALE | | TOTAL | | MALE | | FEMALE | | TOTAL | |
tution	1960	1961	1960	1961	1960	1961	1960	1961	1960	1961	1960	1961
1	59.2	62.1	61.1	58.4	60.0	60.6	40.8	37.9	38.9	41.6	40.0	39.4
2	—	—	57.7	53.9	57.7	53.9	—	—	42.3	46.1	42.3	46.1
3	60.9	64.7	75.2	70.8	65.5	66.7	39.1	35.3	24.8	29.2	34.5	33.3
4	—	—	—	—	—	—	—	—	—	—	—	—
5	80.2	81.3	77.7	86.8	79.3	75.8	19.8	18.7	22.3	13.2	20.7	24.2
6	—	—	—	—	38.9	45.4	—	—	—	—	61.1	54.6
7	20.4	27.1	22.9	35.6	20.8	28.6	79.6	72.9	77.1	64.4	79.2	71.4
8	45.0	39.2	37.3	32.9	42.2	36.9	55.0	60.8	62.7	67.1	57.8	63.1
9	11.6	25.5	23.3	28.0	17.3	26.7	88.4	74.5	76.7	72.0	82.7	73.3
10	48.2	44.4	48.1	46.1	48.0	45.2	51.8	55.6	51.9	53.9	52.0	54.8
11	—	—	46.6	52.3	46.6	52.3	—	—	53.4	47.7	53.4	47.7
12	—	34.4	—	30.3	—	32.3	—	65.6	—	69.7	—	67.7
13	39.8	33.8	47.2	54.1	43.4	42.4	60.2	66.2	52.8	45.9	56.6	57.6
14	61.6	59.3	51.4	48.9	56.9	54.3	38.4	40.7	48.6	51.1	43.1	45.7
15	42.6	43.9	36.6	41.0	40.2	42.7	57.4	56.1	63.4	59.0	59.8	57.3
16	35.6	34.7	36.7	29.4	35.9	32.9	64.4	65.3	63.3	70.6	64.1	67.1
17	—	—	—	—	—	—	—	—	—	—	—	—
18	38.0	30.2	40.3	24.5	39.1	27.6	62.0	69.8	59.7	75.5	60.9	72.4
19	—	—	—	—	—	—	—	—	—	—	—	—
20	61.7	51.2	44.4	53.4	53.4	52.3	38.3	48.8	55.6	46.6	46.6	47.7
21	—	—	—	—	—	—	—	—	—	—	—	—

| | 1960 *Percentages* | | 1961 *Percentages* | |
	RETENTION	WITHDRAWAL	RETENTION	WITHDRAWAL
Male range	11.6–80.2	19.8–88.4	25.5–81.3	18.7–74.5
Median	45.0	55.0	41.5	58.5
Female range	22.9–77.7	22.3–77.1	24.5–86.8	13.2–75.5
Median	46.6	53.4	47.5	52.5
Total range	17.3–79.3	20.7–82.7	26.7–75.8	24.2–73.3
Median	45.0	55.0	45.2	54.8

rate was extremely low,[8] the withdrawal rate has been defined as the percentage of full-time students classified as freshmen in the fall terms of 1960 and 1961 who were not classified as seniors in the fall terms of 1963 and 1964. The retention rate has been defined as the complement of the withdrawal rate. Throughout the study "withdrawal" will

---

[8] Iffert found that the senior year withdrawal rate averaged 6.5 per cent for men and 2.5 per cent for women in liberal arts colleges and 7.3 per cent for all students in all institutions. Iffert, *op. cit.,* p. 16.

be used interchangeably with "attrition" to refer to discontinuance by any full-time student at any time for any reason except graduation.

In these seventeen colleges the median male withdrawal rate only slightly exceeded the median female withdrawal rate for both years. In the 1960 entering class this difference was 1.6 per cent and in the 1961 group, 6.0 per cent. The literature seems to indicate that the four-year withdrawal rates are approximately the same for both men and women and the present data tend to support that conclusion. The range from the institution with the highest to the institution with the lowest withdrawal rates reflects the findings of the Summerskill review of thirty-five studies which showed a range from 12 per cent to 82 per cent.[9] The withdrawal rates in the present study are not comparable to those of previous studies due to the omission of the senior class withdrawals, but their wide range is evident. Table 2 illustrates the gross withdrawal rates for twenty of the colleges in the 1963–64 academic year and reflects the percentage of full-time students enrolled in the fall term of 1963 who were not enrolled in the fall term of 1964. The term "gross attrition" refers to the withdrawal of *all* full-time students who leave the institution voluntarily or involuntarily within a stated period of time. All computations have been based on actual numbers of students; percentages of women or of men have been based on the total number of women or of men, rather than on the total number of all students.

The male and female gross attrition rates (Table 2) have a narrower range than the withdrawal rates for a single class over a three-year period (Table 1). As indicated in Table 2, the percentage of all students who withdrew ranged from 11.6 per cent to 37.5 per cent. The median gross attrition rate for all students in the colleges studied was 18.1 per cent and the median male rate exceeded the female by 2.3 per cent. Thus there is little difference between the median male and the median female gross attrition rates in these twenty institutions, a finding also true of the withdrawal rate of the classes presented in Table 1.

It is revealing to examine more closely the gross attrition rates through an analysis of voluntary and nonvoluntary withdrawals. The term "voluntary withdrawal" signifies discontinuance by those full-time students, including transfer students and students with physical or mental illnesses, who, according to the official institutional records, withdrew of their own volition. Where the term "nonvoluntary withdrawal" is used, it refers to discontinuance by full-time students entered on institutional records as ineligible to continue for academic or disciplinary reasons.

[9] Summerskill, *op. cit.,* p. 630.

TABLE 2. GROSS WITHDRAWAL RATES FOR FULL-TIME STUDENTS ENROLLED IN
TWENTY COLLEGES IN FALL TERM 1963 WHO WERE NOT ENROLLED IN
FALL TERM 1964

| *Institution* | Percentages | | |
	MALE	FEMALE	TOTAL
1	15.3	11.1	13.5
2	—	12.2	12.2
3	14.4	5.3	11.6
5	22.1	7.6	16.0
6	19.9	16.9	18.5
7	30.9	28.1	30.3
8	17.2	21.6	17.2
9	10.3	14.1	12.0
10	24.9	20.6	23.0
11	—	14.3	14.3
12	25.2	17.6	21.7
13	20.3	15.1	18.9
14	18.2	17.9	18.1
15	19.2	19.0	19.1
16	28.2	32.3	29.5
17	17.0	16.9	17.0
18	26.5	22.6	24.8
19	16.3	18.7	17.6
20	36.1	39.2	37.5
21	17.8	16.6	18.0

	Percentage range
Male range	10.3–36.1
Median	19.6
Female range	5.3–39.2
Median	17.3
Total range	11.6–37.5
Median	18.1

As indicated in Table 3, withdrawal rates for students leaving the
institution for nonvoluntary reasons ranged from 0.2 per cent to 16.4,
with a median of 5.4 per cent. In comparison, the voluntary withdrawal rate was much greater with a range of 5.3 to 34.5 per cent, and
a median more than double that of the nonvoluntary withdrawals.

The range of percentages of male nonvoluntary withdrawals was
twice that of the female, and the male median percentage was about
two and one-half that of the female. It is obvious, then, that a higher

TABLE 3. NONVOLUNTARY AND VOLUNTARY WITHDRAWAL RATES FOR FULL-TIME
STUDENTS ENROLLED IN TWENTY COLLEGES IN FALL TERM 1963 WHO WERE NOT
ENROLLED IN FALL TERM 1964

	Nonvoluntary percentages			Voluntary percentages		
Institution	MALE	FEMALE	TOTAL	MALE	FEMALE	TOTAL
1	3.6	5.3	2.3	11.6	10.6	11.2
2	—	3.6	3.6	—	8.2	8.2
3	8.6	0.8	6.2	5.7	4.4	5.3
5	12.2	2.9	8.2	9.9	4.7	7.7
6	4.7	1.6	3.3	15.1	15.2	15.2
7	18.6	8.5	16.4	12.3	20.1	13.8
8	6.1	3.4	5.1	6.1	18.1	13.6
9	1.8	0.5	1.2	8.4	13.6	10.7
10	8.0	2.6	5.7	16.8	18.0	17.3
11	—	3.2	3.2	—	11.0	11.0
12	8.1	1.5	5.1	17.0	16.0	16.5
13	11.1	2.5	7.1	9.2	14.6	11.8
14	12.2	8.7	10.6	6.0	9.2	7.5
15	0.2	—	0.2	18.9	19.0	18.9
16	16.7	9.0	14.2	11.4	23.3	15.2
17	7.8	3.2	5.5	9.2	13.7	11.4
18	10.9	2.7	7.2	15.6	19.9	17.5
19	7.7	8.4	8.1	8.6	10.3	9.5
20	3.9	1.8	2.9	32.1	37.3	34.5
21	5.6	3.7	4.8	12.2	14.6	13.2

	Percentage ranges	
	NONVOLUNTARY	VOLUNTARY
Male range	0.2–18.6	5.7–32.1
Median	7.9	11.5
Female range	0.5–9.0	4.4–37.3
Median	3.2	14.6
Total range	0.2–16.4	5.3–34.5
Median	5.4	12.5

percentage of the men than of the women left these colleges involuntarily.

On the other hand, the range of percentages as well as the median percentage of female voluntary withdrawals exceeded that of the male withdrawals. Thus a greater percentage of the women enrolled than of the men left the twenty colleges voluntarily. This condition confirms the findings of Iffert and those reported by Summerskill.

STUDENT POPULATION

The participating colleges furnished a list of 2,037 students who had voluntarily withdrawn between September 1963 and September 1964. This number represented 12.6 per cent of all students enrolled during that period and was divided almost equally between men and women. All the students were academically successful up to the time of withdrawal and there has been little concern with high school records, percentile ranking or placement tests, or other measurements which have often been correlated with success in college.

A questionnaire was mailed to each student concerning his background, his perceptions of his institution while he was there, and the influence of these perceptions on his decision to withdraw. Responses to the questionnaire indicated that many students associated the term "withdraw" exclusively with discontinuance of college level work. As a result, many, feeling that the study included only college dropouts and not students who transferred, did not complete the questionnaire. Nevertheless, valid responses were received from 54.1 per cent of the total population of 2,037 students. The responses are slightly skewed toward women in that 57.35 per cent of the returns were from women and 42.65 per cent were from men.

Many questionnaires were returned with letters or comments expressing support for this type of research and offering to provide additional information. Over one-half of the students responding added comments in the space provided for that purpose. Moreover, letters containing additional information also were received from students and parents.

It was found that at the time of withdrawal 35 per cent of the respondents were freshmen, 40 per cent were sophomores, 18 per cent were juniors, and 3 per cent were seniors. An additional 4 per cent did not indicate their class standing at the time of withdrawal. Eleven per cent of the entire group spent less than one full year at the college, 40 per cent completed one full year, 34 per cent were at their college of first enrollment for two full years, 10 per cent were there for three full years, and 1 per cent withdrew after four full years. Again, 4 per cent failed to supply the information. While the majority of students withdrew at the end of a term, 3 per cent withdrew during the first two weeks of a term, 7 per cent during the middle of a term, and 10 per cent during the last two weeks of a term.

Iffert found that transfers and dropouts occur with the greatest frequency during the first two years, with nearly 40 per cent occurring during the first year, and 83 per cent occurring by the end of the second year.[10] In these percentages he referred to total nonvoluntary and volun-

[10] Iffert, *op. cit.,* p. 105.

tary withdrawals, whereas the present study is concerned only with voluntary withdrawals. However, the respondents to the current study seem to mirror the proportion found by Iffert in that about 85 per cent withdrew by the end of the first two full years.

With the exception of approximately twenty-one students who delayed entrance for more than two years beyond high school, all respondents were of college age. The literature seems to indicate that age as such does not affect attrition, although older undergraduates may fall victim to the same personal or financial problems that caused them to delay their entrance.

The average respondent was one of two or three children. Fifteen per cent indicated that they had one or more brothers or sisters of college age not attending college. Twenty-five per cent had brothers or sisters attending college, while the same percentage had brothers or sisters who had completed college.

It was found that the homes of two-thirds of the respondents were located beyond convenient daily traveling distance to the colleges. This percentage approximates Iffert's findings on this point. Iffert concluded that the location of his home has no significant bearing on a student's chances for graduation.[11]

The majority of respondents in this study lived in college housing at the time they withdrew. Iffert found that students who lived in college dormitories or other college-operated facilities had the best average persistence record, though their persistence was affected by other factors. In the present study 72.8 per cent of the respondents reported they shared rooms with other students. Sixty-three and eight-tenths per cent reportedly had one roommate, 6 per cent had two roommates, and 3 per cent shared rooms with three roommates.

SOCIOECONOMIC BACKGROUND

As pointed out above, research findings concerning the effect of socioeconomic background factors on attrition are equivocal.[12] However, because the influence of socioeconomic factors depends on the college environment, it may be useful for colleges of the kind included in this study to have some knowledge of the backgrounds of their voluntary dropouts. At any rate, one section of the questionnaire was designed to gather socioeconomic background information.

Table 4 lists the occupational categories of the respondents' fathers. The "Not known or no response" category has a wide range because a large proportion of the respondents in some colleges reported their

[11] *Ibid.*, p. 74.
[12] Summerskill, *op. cit.*, p. 632.

TABLE 4. OCCUPATIONS OF FATHERS

Categories	Percentages of 1102 respondents	Range of percentages of respondents in 21 colleges
Professional	24.57	5.00–42.42
Minister	2.18	1.19– 6.67
Managerial or proprietary	24.75	4.41–38.18
Farm owner or manager	7.71	2.63–27.85
Semi-professional—technician	6.07	1.37–10.00
Clerical and sales	6.98	1.47–24.24
Skilled (computers, etc.)	7.52	2.63–14.06
Semi-skilled (mechanic)	7.16	2.04–27.78
Unskilled (laborer)	4.90	1.47–35.00
Not known or no response	8.16	1.75–30.00

fathers' occupations, while in others the majority did not give this information.

Parents' educational level can influence the success of students in that students tend to reflect the educational values held by their parents. Those from families where the father has studied beyond the baccalaureate degree and the mother beyond the high school level tend to achieve more than their admission credentials would suggest. Table 5 lists the percentage of respondents reporting their parents' highest level of formal education in each category.

As would be expected, a very low percentage of the parents (less than 17 per cent of the fathers and 13 per cent of the mothers) failed to graduate from high school. Nearly one-fourth of the fathers and one-third of the mothers made the secondary school diploma a terminal point. More than half of the parents were admitted to college, but only one-third of the fathers and one-fourth of the mothers remained in college to receive degrees. Slightly less than one-sixth of the fathers and slightly more than one-twentieth of the mothers earned graduate degrees.

Thus within the total responding group a significant proportion (over 12 per cent) of the students have at least one parent who has not graduated from high school. However, the parents of over 25 per cent finished high school but went no further, those of over 50 per cent entered college, those of over 24 per cent received a college degree, those of over 6 per cent received a graduate degree, and lastly, the parents of over 20 per cent of the students dropped out of college themselves.

While gross income is one measure of the family's ability to support a student's higher education, this figure must be considered in the light of other factors such as the number and ages of siblings, the type of

TABLE 5.   HIGHEST LEVEL OF PARENTS' FORMAL EDUCATION

Level of education	Percentages of 1102 respondents	
	FATHER	MOTHER
Elementary school	3.81	2.63
Junior high school	6.26	3.36
Ninth through eleventh grade	6.17	6.90
Twelfth grade or high school graduate	24.77	31.34
Less than one year of college	4.63	4.45
One to three years of college	15.52	21.98
College graduate (Bachelor's degree)	17.42	19.07
Professional degree (M.D., Law, etc.)	8.62	1.91
Master's degree	6.26	3.27
Doctorate (Ph.D., Ed.D., etc.)	1.36	0.27
No response	5.18	4.82

institution attended, and the subject field of interest, all of which bear on family support patterns.

Iffert found that the quality of college students as measured by placement tests was not related to family income.[13] He concluded that the difference between the median family income of dropouts and that of students who persist to graduation was significant and related to attrition because lack of money is a major reason for student dropouts. Iffert also observed that the median family income of students in private colleges was significantly higher than that of those in public colleges. The students from private, non-church-related colleges had the highest median income, those from Roman Catholic church-related colleges ranked second and those from non-Catholic church-related institutions ranked third.[14]

Table 6 indicates the students' estimates of their family's total gross income for 1963, and the range for the twenty-one colleges.

Over one-half of the family gross incomes falls between $5,000 and $12,999, with the highest percentage in the $9,000 to $10,000 bracket. The differences in individual colleges are again evident in the range for each income bracket.

Most studies list lack of funds as one of the three principal reasons given by students for withdrawing. Such findings are usually qualified with statements that this reason for withdrawal is socially accepted and therefore often used to disguise other more important reasons. The literature also states that self-support and part-time work are poor factors for predicting success or failure in college.

[13] Iffert, *op. cit.*, p. 61.
[14] *Ibid.*, p. 64.

TABLE 6. FAMILY'S GROSS INCOME

Gross income 1963	Percentages of 1102 respondents	Range of percentages of respondents in 21 colleges
$21,000 and over	12.52	3.03–29.73
19,000–20,999	3.54	1.61–9.59
17,000–18,999	2.81	1.27–9.09
15,000–16,999	6.26	2.04–12.90
13,000–14,999	4.81	1.61–12.31
11,000–12,999	11.98	2.70–22.22
9,000–10,999	15.61	5.41–28.57
7,000–8,999	11.89	2.04–22.22
5,000–6,999	11.71	2.70–20.00
3,000–4,999	4.26	1.37–35.00
0–2,999	1.72	.87–9.09
No response	12.89	

In the current study, questionnaire responses revealed that over 56 per cent of the women and over 36 per cent of the men received nearly all their financial support from their parents. Over 76 per cent of the women and over 63 per cent of the men received at least one-half of their financial support from parents, while scholarships furnished some income for 20 per cent of the men and 26 per cent of the women. In general, scholarships provide from 10 to 20 per cent of the recipients' support.

The percentage of women receiving money from loans was slightly above the percentage of men, 17 and 14 per cent, respectively. The majority of both men and women receiving loans acquired in this way an amount equal to between 10 and 30 per cent of their total expenses.

To the question, "Are you a member of a religious denomination," nearly 88 per cent of the respondents said "yes" and approximately 8 per cent said "no." Another 4 per cent left this item blank. This question was followed by an item that asked if the college has a religious affiliation, and, if so, if it was the same as the respondent's. Thirty-one per cent indicated "yes" and approximately 51 per cent said "no," while a number of respondents did not answer this question. Some, apparently realizing that an answer would be, in effect, a statement of their own religious affiliation, replied, ". . . it is none of your business."

REASONS FOR GOING TO COLLEGE

Many writers have supported the idea that a student's chances of remaining in college are positively related to the strength of his motivation. No examination of withdrawal should fail to consider students'

TABLE 7.   REASONS FOR GOING TO COLLEGE RATED "OF GREAT IMPORTANCE"

	Percentages of 1102 respondents		
Reasons	WOMEN (632)	MEN (470)	TOTAL
I felt a college degree was necessary for the kind of work I wanted to do.	62.18	61.32	61.80
I wanted to prepare myself for a better paying job than I would otherwise be able to get.	35.92	46.58	40.77
It had always been expected that I would go to college.	37.34	28.21	33.39
I wanted to find out more about certain fields of knowledge.	39.88	23.29	32.49
I enjoy studying and wanted to continue academic work.	31.49	10.90	22.69
I hoped that college training would enable me to be a better husband or wife.	26.74	8.33	18.87
I had serious intellectual curiosities which only college could satisfy.	22.15	13.89	18.60
My teachers thought I was good college material.	18.99	11.11	13.61
Most of my friends were going to college.	11.23	7.48	9.62
I thought a college education would enable me to be more influential in community affairs.	5.70	6.84	6.17

reasons for going to college. Consequently, the questionnaire included ten reasons for going to college selected from a list of twenty-five developed by Iffert.[15] Respondents were asked to indicate the level of importance of each reason as it influenced their decisions to attend college, and to add to the list if their reason was not included among the options.

Table 7 presents the ten reasons in the order of descending significance based on the percentage of respondents judging the item "of great importance." Because individual respondents may have thought more than one item "of great importance," the percentages shown total far more than 100 per cent.

Iffert divided his twenty-five reasons for going to college into five categories: academic, occupational, personal-self, social service, and traditional. In discussing the respondents' choices it may prove helpful to think of them in terms of Iffert's categories.

A comparison of individual items reveals the occupational item, "I felt a college degree was necessary for the kind of work I wanted to do,"

[15] Ibid., pp. 22-23.

to have been rated "of great importance" by the largest percentage of both men and women. The reason in second place in terms of total respondents, rated second by men and fourth by women, is the occupational item, "I wanted to prepare myself for a better paying job than I would otherwise be able to get." Thus, although men and women had different rating patterns, occupational reasons were considered "of great importance" by both sexes significantly more often than were reasons in other categories.

Iffert found that women in liberal arts colleges rated academic reasons first as factors in their decisions to attend college, while men rated them second. The present study reveals a trend in this direction because the item receiving the second largest percentage of women's choices, "I wanted to find out more about certain fields of knowledge," falls in the academic category. This item was fourth in order of choice by men. Women also rated three additional academic category items relatively high. Thirty-one per cent, 22 per cent, and 19 per cent of women reported these three items "of great importance," while about half these percentages of men chose them.

The traditional item, "It had always been expected that I would go to college," was ranked third in importance by both men and women. The personal-self reason, "I hoped that college training would enable me to be a better husband or wife," ranked sixth in importance in the list of ten, but only 8 per cent of the men, compared with 27 per cent of the women, thought it "of great importance." Two items from the social service category appeared in ninth and tenth places on the list, indicating that a rather small percentage of respondents considered them significant influences on their decision to attend college.

Iffert concluded that the relative importance of the categories of reasons for going to college did not vary significantly with the type of institutional support or control and that no significant relationship existed between the students' reasons for going to college and the length of their stay in college.[16] No attempt has been made in this study to relate reasons for going to college to persistence.

The most significant finding of this part of the study was that women are apparently more inclined to attend college for academic and personal reasons than are men. However, both men and women are chiefly concerned with occupational goals and later specialization.

STUDENT REACTIONS TO COLLEGE FACILITIES AND SERVICES

The present study was also designed to determine student reactions to experiences related to the various services, facilities, and, by implica-

[16] *Ibid.*, pp. 31, 34.

TABLE 8. FACILITIES AND SERVICES: TEN ITEMS RATED SATISFACTORY OR
UNSATISFACTORY BY HIGHEST PERCENTAGE OF 1102 RESPONDENTS

Items	Percentages of 1102 respondents
SATISFACTORY	
Size of my classes (I.P.)	85.7
Services of the admissions office prior to enrollment (G.A.S.)	82.4
*Opportunity to have private conferences with instructors on academic questions stemming from course work (F.-S.R.)	78.4
*Opportunity to consult from time to time with my major adviser (F.-S.R.)	78.4
*Opportunity to participate in organized student activities (S.P.S.)	78.4
Teaching abilities of my instructors (F.-S.R.)	77.9
*Opportunity for informal social contacts with students (C.-C.E.)	75.9
General type of student attending the college (C.-C.E.)	73.8
*Opportunities for religious life (C.-C.E.)	72.1
*Opportunities to select adequate housing (S.P.S.)	71.4
UNSATISFACTORY	
*Recreational facilities in town (C.-C.E.)	64.5
Recreational facilities on campus (C.-C.E.)	47.1
*Services of my faculty adviser in helping me select my first term courses (F.-S.R.)	41.8
Degree of emphasis in college on vocational guidance (S.P.S.)	41.5
*Assistance from counselors on "how to study" techniques (S.P.S.)	41.4
*Compulsory chapel and assembly attendance (G.A.S.)	39.0
Services of student health department (G.A.S.)	38.8
Study conditions in the library (G.A.S.)	37.9
*Assistance from instructors on "how to study" techniques (F.-S.R.)	35.7
College rules relating to social activities (S.P.S.)	35.1

* Items which appear in a similar listing by Iffert, *op. cit.*, p. 36.

Explanation of abbreviations following items:
   G.A.S.—General Administrative Services
   S.P.S.—Student Personnel Services
   F.-S.R.—Faculty-Student Relations
   I.P.—Instructional Program
   C.-C.E.—College-Community Environment

tion, personnel of the college. Students were asked to indicate their level of satisfaction with each of fifty-one items, the majority of which were used in the Iffert study reported in 1957.[17]

The questionnaire presented a choice of four levels of satisfaction, ranging from very unsatisfactory to very satisfactory. Within these extremes were included the intermediate possibilities—somewhat un-

[17] *Ibid.*, pp. 36–38.

satisfactory and fairly satisfactory. An additional choice, "does not apply to me, or no opinion," was also included. The percentages of satisfactory and unsatisfactory responses which appear on Tables 9 through 13 were derived by combining the "very satisfactory" with the "fairly satisfactory" responses, and the "very unsatisfactory" with the "somewhat unsatisfactory."

Because there appeared to be no significant difference between the responses of males and of females, they were combined for this analysis. Where possible, findings have been compared with those in the Iffert study; however, Iffert's analysis of similar data was based only on the responses of male graduates because he, too, found little difference between the responses of men and of women or between those of graduates and nongraduates.[18]

In the following discussion of student reactions, if more than 25 per cent of the respondents considered an item unsatisfactory, the facilities and services represented by that item will be arbitrarily regarded as unsatisfactory, even if more than 25 per cent took an opposing view.

Ten items most frequently rated satisfactory and ten most frequently judged unsatisfactory are presented in descending order in Table 8. Reference to this table will be made from time to time.

For analysis and discussion the responses have been grouped into five categories: general administrative services, student personnel services, faculty-student relations, instructional program, and college-community environment.

GENERAL ADMINISTRATIVE SERVICES

Table 9 presents respondents' reactions to the general administrative services at these colleges. The items are arranged in descending order based on percentages of satisfactory responses. "Services of the admissions office prior to enrollment" stands at the top of the list with the highest percentage of satisfactory and the lowest percentage of unsatisfactory ratings. "Services of the registrar's office" received the second highest percentage of satisfactory responses and "Services of the business office" received the fourth highest percentage of satisfactory ratings. Because about 50 per cent of the respondents had attended the institution for one year or less, they had recent experience on which to base their ratings of these offices. Iffert determined that "Services of the registrar's office" was rated satisfactory by a greater percentage of students in church-related institutions than in publicly controlled institutions and private institutions independent of church.[19]

[18] *Ibid.,* p. 35.
[19] *Ibid.,* p. 40.

TABLE 9. GENERAL ADMINISTRATIVE SERVICES:
STUDENTS' RATINGS OF COLLEGE FACILITIES AND SERVICES

Items	Percentages of 1102 respondents indicating		
	SATIS-FACTORY	UNSATIS-FACTORY	NO OPINION
Services of the admissions office prior to enrollment	82.4	7.4	4.9
Services of the registrar's office	69.6	18.0	6.9
College rules governing academic life, such as class cuts	69.5	24.4	2.2
Services of the business office	63.4	16.1	15.0
Study conditions in the library	54.0	37.9	2.8
Assistance from academic deans on problems related to course work	40.6	26.5	27.5
Compulsory chapel and assembly attendance	39.4	39.4	16.0
Services of student health department	39.0	38.8	16.2
Opportunity to compete for scholarship aid	34.6	13.1	47.0

NOTE: Percentages do not total 100 since "no response" figures are not shown.

Three types of administrative services—"Services of the student health department," "Compulsory chapel and assembly attendance," and "Study conditions in the library"—were rated unsatisfactory by over 38 per cent of the respondents. These items appear in Table 8 on the list of ten most frequently ranked unsatisfactory. The "Compulsory chapel and assembly attendance" item also appears on Iffert's list of items most frequently ranked unsatisfactory.[20]

When asked to rate their level of satisfaction with "Opportunity to compete for scholarship aid," a great number of respondents indicated "no opinion" or that the item did not apply. The 34.6 per cent who rated this item satisfactory is close to the 25 per cent who indicated they received some income from scholarship sources.

The general administrative services category includes one item among the ten most often rated satisfactory and three among those most frequently rated unsatisfactory. The three unsatisfactory areas were health services, study conditions in the library, and compulsory chapel and assembly attendance. Over 35 per cent of the respondents showed some level of dissatisfaction with these three types of services. This is not to say that 35 per cent of these students withdrew for these reasons, but unsatisfactory experiences with such facilities and services could have been contributing factors. Almost 27 per cent of the respondents indicated dissatisfaction with "Assistance from academic

[20] *Ibid.*, p. 39.

TABLE 10. STUDENT PERSONNEL SERVICES:
STUDENTS' RATINGS OF COLLEGE FACILITIES AND SERVICES

Items	Percentages of 1102 respondents indicating		
	SATIS-FACTORY	UNSATIS-FACTORY	NO OPINION
Opportunity to participate in organized student activities	78.4*	10.5	5.6
Opportunity to secure adequate housing	71.4*	10.1	13.2
Orientation program at start of Freshman year	59.9	25.5	8.9
Opportunity to consult with personnel deans (dean of students, dean of women, dean of men) on personal problems	59.1	20.5	14.9
Study conditions in my room	55.1	33.1	6.4
College rules relating to social activities	54.4	35.1*	4.8
Opportunity to receive help on important spiritual and moral problems	51.5	18.0	23.1
Quality of help generally available from personnel deans	49.0	27.1	18.3
Quality of counseling assistance received on problems of educational and vocational choices	42.0	33.1	19.4
Opportunity to get testing and counseling to help determine educational and vocational goals	39.6	30.0	25.1
Availability of occupational information for help in choosing an occupation	38.4	29.8	26.0
Degree of emphasis in college on vocational guidance	33.6	41.5*	18.9
Opportunity to secure loans from the college	31.7	12.7	49.2
Assistance from college officials in obtaining part-time employment	29.1	12.5	53.1
Assistance from counselors on "how to study" techniques	24.7	41.4*	28.4

* Included in listings of ten highest rated satisfactory, unsatisfactory.
NOTE: Percentages do not total 100 since "no response" figures are not shown.

deans on course work problems." By the criterion stated above, this service would receive an unsatisfactory rating.

STUDENT PERSONNEL SERVICES

Of the items related to student personnel services on Table 10, two—"Opportunity to secure adequate housing" and "Opportunity to participate in organized student activities outside the classroom"—fell among the ten most frequently rated satisfactory. These two items were also included in the ten items most frequently rated satisfactory in the

Iffert study. Three items included among the services most often rated unsatisfactory in the present study concern "College rules relating to social activities, "Assistance from counselors on 'how-to-study' techniques," and "Degree of emphasis in college on vocational guidance." The latter two items also appeared on Iffert's list of the ten items most commonly rated unsatisfactory.

The unsatisfactory ratings given to items such as "Degree of emphasis in college on vocational guidance," "Opportunity to get testing and counseling to help determine educational and vocational goals," "Availability of occupational information for help in choosing an occupation," and "Quality of counseling assistance received on problems of educational and vocational choices" evidence a need for increased attention to such services. The whole college program should not be centered on occupational goals, but students should be able to discuss vocational matters with informed persons and be able to avoid the situation described by one student who said:

> At the end of my Freshman year I felt that a liberal arts degree was a senseless one to have since it was not preparing me for any specific [job]. Also I had no idea of what I wanted to be. After 1½ years at [a larger university] and looking back, I feel that I should have graduated with a liberal arts degree, then taken up hotel work at the graduate level.

Thus, although items related to counseling on personal or spiritual problems were rated satisfactory, those items dealing with educational and vocational counseling were rated unsatisfactory. As a whole, the level of satisfaction with student personnel services averaged below that of the other four categories.

FACULTY-STUDENT RELATIONS

On Table 11 respondents indicated a relatively high degree of satisfaction with the following items: "Teaching abilities of instructors," "Opportunity to have private conferences with instructors on academic questions stemming from course work," and "Opportunity to consult from time to time during freshman year with faculty adviser." All three were among the ten items most often rated satisfactory in this study and the latter two were among the ten items most frequently ranked satisfactory in the Iffert study. The ratings given to these and similar items—including "Opportunity to have private conferences with instructors on personal questions stemming from course work," and "Opportunity to consult from time to time during freshman year with faculty adviser"—indicate that the students were generally satisfied with their relations with the faculty.

TABLE 11. FACULTY-STUDENT RELATIONS:
STUDENTS' RATINGS OF COLLEGE FACILITIES AND SERVICES

Items	Percentages of 1102 respondents indicating		
	SATIS-FACTORY	UNSATIS-FACTORY	NO OPINION
Opportunity to have private conferences with instructors on academic questions stemming from course work	78.4*	10.6	5.9
Opportunity to consult from time to time with major adviser	78.4*	10.5	5.6
Teaching abilities of my instructors	77.9*	15.8	1.1
Opportunity to have private conferences with instructors on personal questions stemming from course work	66.0	12.5	16.2
Opportunity to consult from time to time during Freshman year with faculty adviser	61.6	20.1	13.1
Opportunity for informal social contacts with faculty	58.7	25.7	10.4
Quality of help usually available from major adviser	54.5	26.9	13.4
Services of my faculty adviser in helping me select my first term courses	45.9	41.8*	7.1
Assistance from instructors on "how to study" techniques	37.0	35.7*	21.9

* Included in listings of ten highest rated satisfactory, unsatisfactory.
NOTE: Percentages do not total 100 since "no response" figures are not shown.

Despite this general satisfaction, there are four items relating to student-faculty relations which were considered unsatisfactory in the present investigation. Three of these items concern educational counseling and are related to the educational counseling items in the Student Personnel Services category which also received unsatisfactory ratings. Two of the three—"Assistance from instructors on 'how-to-study' techniques" and "Services of faculty adviser in helping select first-term courses"— appear on the list of the ten items with the highest percentages of unsatisfactory ratings in this study as well as in Iffert's. Thus, there seems to be a need for more time and effort in orienting the student to program requirements and study skills.

INSTRUCTIONAL PROGRAM

"Size of classes" received the highest level of satisfactory ratings of any item in the category of college services and facilities presented in Table 12. Iffert determined that students in junior colleges were most satisfied with class size, that those in teachers colleges and liberal arts

TABLE 12. INSTRUCTIONAL PROGRAM:
STUDENTS' RATINGS OF COLLEGE FACILITIES AND SERVICES

Items	Percentages of 1102 respondents indicating		
	SATIS-FACTORY	UNSATIS-FACTORY	NO OPINION
Size of my classes	85.7*	7.0	2.0
Ability of instructors to set forth clear-cut and interesting course objectives	67.0	25.6	1.9
Services and facilities of the library	65.7	27.7	1.5
Opportunity to take elective courses along with required program	64.2	26.0	4.3
Availability of courses and facilities for training in my major field	56.5	30.0	8.6

* Included in listings of ten highest rated satisfactory, unsatisfactory.
NOTE: Percentages do not total 100 since "no response" figures are not shown.

colleges were almost tied for second place, while students in technological institutions were fourth, and those in universities were least satisfied with class size.[21] Since satisfaction with class size was rated so high, it was not a significant factor in students' decisions to withdraw from the colleges in this study.

"Ability of instructors to set forth clear-cut and interesting course objectives" was rated unsatisfactory by almost 26 per cent of those responding. However, this rating is perhaps balanced by the strongly satisfactory rating given to "Teaching abilities of my instructors," presented on Table 11.

"Services and facilities of the library" was rated unsatisfactory by nearly 28 per cent of the respondents. This rating might have been predicted on the basis of the almost 38 per cent on Table 9 who expressed dissatisfaction with "Study conditions in the library." "Opportunity to take elective courses along with required program" was rated unsatisfactory by 26 per cent of the respondents, but no student commented on course requirements as a factor contributing to his decision to withdraw.

"Availability of courses and facilities for training in my major field" was rated unsatisfactory by 30 per cent of the respondents. Although this was the item rated lowest among those concerning the instructional program, it is not among the ten items most often rated unsatisfactory. Nevertheless, the students' lack of satisfaction with courses and facilities for training in the major field is evident in comments such as that of the young man who wrote, "As I moved into more advanced courses I

[21] *Ibid.*, pp. 42–43.

TABLE 13. College-community Environment:
Students' Ratings of College Facilities and Services

| | Percentages of 1102 respondents indicating | | |
Items	SATIS-FACTORY	UNSATIS-FACTORY	NO OPINION
Opportunity for informal social contacts with students	75.9*	16.0	2.5
General type of students attending the college	73.8*	18.6	1.7
Opportunities for religious life	72.1*	8.8	13.1
Customs and practices regarding campus apparel	70.4	17.6	6.2
General intellectual life around the college	64.4	26.4	1.4
Treatment by townspeople	64.3	19.4	10.3
Degree of emphasis in college on intellectual and cultural pursuits outside the classroom	60.8	28.6	4.9
Opportunities for dating	60.2	26.6	7.2
Emphasis on intercollegiate athletics	52.6	27.8	13.3
Opportunity to join a fraternal group of my liking	45.8	16.2	32.3
Recreational facilities on campus	44.5	47.1*	3.0
Hazing by students	44.4	13.9	35.3
Emphasis on social fraternities (sororities)	38.2	28.4	27.2
Recreational facilities in the town	21.1	64.5*	8.5

* Included in listings of ten highest rated satisfactory, unsatisfactory.
Note: Percentages do not total 100 since "no response" figures are not shown.

discovered the courses and instructors were not as advertised, so I transferred to [a larger school] with a strong department."

COLLEGE-COMMUNITY ENVIRONMENT

Three of the four items which top the list of those concerned with college-community environment on Table 13 were also among the items most often rated satisfactory in the entire study. In addition, three of these four items also appeared in Iffert's listing of the ten most satisfactory items revealed in his study. The first of these items concerns "Opportunity for informal social contacts with students" and could be related to the high level of satisfaction with the second item, "General type of student attending the college." Iffert found that satisfaction with other students attending the college was significantly higher in church-related institutions than in other institutions and that, when coupled with high ratings on similar items, these data seem to indicate that students in church-related colleges are better pleased with their fellow students than are students elsewhere.[22] The third most satisfactory college-com-

[22] *Ibid.*, p. 40.

munity environment item in the present study concerned "Opportunities for religious life" and was first among the ten items most often rated satisfactory in the Iffert study. Iffert found that students from church-related and public colleges gave this item the highest average rating while it was ranked third in privately controlled institutions independent of church.[23] The fourth item sought reactions to "Customs and practices regarding campus apparel" and revealed a high level of satisfaction, as in the Iffert study.

Over 26 per cent of the respondents gave the item on "General intellectual life around the college" an unsatisfactory rating, and an even larger percentage was dissatisfied with the "Degree of emphasis in college on intellectual and cultural pursuits outside the classroom." An item similar to the latter was ranked tenth among the ten most unsatisfactory items in the Iffert study.[24]

Nineteen per cent of the present respondents indicated no participation in extracurricular activities, 29 per cent indicated some participation, and 47 per cent indicated active participation. There was little difference between the amount of participation reported by males and that reported by females. It is generally believed that participation in extracurricular activities does not affect attrition, but Iffert found that fraternity or sorority membership, on the other hand, was clearly associated with persistence to graduation.[25] He found that students who were members or pledges of fraternities or sororities had better persistence and graduation records in the institutions of first registration than did nonmembers. Also, institutions having local or national social fraternities and sororities had lower withdrawal rates than institutions without these organizations.[26] He noted, however, that ". . . This is a statement of finding, not a statement of causal relationship."[27] At any rate, the percentage of respondents expressing dissatisfaction with "Opportunity to join a fraternal group of my liking" was small, indicating that most of the respondents who desired such membership were granted this opportunity. A related item—"Emphasis on social fraternities (sororities)"—was thought unsatisfactory by more than 28 per cent of the respondents. However, the word "emphasis" is somewhat ambiguous, and it is uncertain if the respondents' dissatisfaction stemmed from too much or too little emphasis on fraternities and sororities.

"Emphasis on intercollegiate athletics" was found unsatisfactory by

[23] *Ibid.*, p. 38.
[24] *Ibid.*, p. 39.
[25] *Ibid.*, p. 80.
[26] *Ibid.*
[27] *Ibid.*, p. 77.

almost 28 per cent of the respondents. The use of the word "emphasis" again makes it difficult to determine whether more or less emphasis is desired.

Two items from the college-community environment were among the ten most frequently rated unsatisfactory in this study and also appeared in Iffert's list of the ten items most often rated unsatisfactory. Both are concerned with recreational facilities. "Recreational facilities on campus" was rated unsatisfactory by approximately 47 per cent of the respondents and "Recreational facilities in the town" was rated unsatisfactory by nearly 65 per cent. A related item, "Opportunities for dating," was found unsatisfactory by almost 27 per cent of the respondents. On the other hand, an item on "Treatment by townspeople" revealed a general satisfaction. These ratings show that students actually evaluated the recreational facilities as unsatisfactory, but were highly satisfied with their treatment by townspeople.

Three of the items concerning the college-community environment were among those most often rated satisfactory and two were among those most often rated unsatisfactory. The respondents seemed satisfied with the student body, and the religious opportunities, but they were dissatisfied with the recreational facilities on the campus and in the community.

FACILITIES AND SERVICES—SUMMARY

Composite percentages within each of the five categories ranked the instructional program most satisfactory, faculty-student relations next, college-community environment third, general administrative services fourth, and student personnel services last. The differences between the rankings are slight, and the categories into which the items were divided might be disputed. The composite student judgments were generally consistent, however, and tend to confirm the validity of the ratings. Thus when a specific service or facility received a very high or low rating, related services or facilities tended to be rated at the same level of satisfaction.

A large percentage of students generally gave satisfactory ratings to items connected with the academic program, the student body, and the administrative services of the college. However, the responses evidenced a significant amount of dissatisfaction with the counseling, guidance, and orientation services, and a high degree of dissatisfaction with the availability of adequate recreational facilities on and off campus.

Iffert analyzed student responses to questions regarding college facilities and services by dividing them into three areas of responsibility:

administration, nonacademic deans, and faculty.[28] He found that the services normally considered to be primarily the responsibility of the administration received the highest ratings, those usually considered to be the function of the nonacademic deans were rated second, and those representing the faculty areas of operation were rated lowest. When the items in the present study were grouped in this way for comparative purposes, a different rating order emerged. Administration ranked first, as in the Iffert study, but faculty areas of operation were second, while matters handled by the nonacademic deans were last. The ranking obtained in the present study does not indicate any weakening of the nonacademic deans' functions, but it shows the difference between the over-all ratings of faculty by students in all the types of institutions studied by Iffert and the somewhat higher ratings of faculty by students in these small liberal arts colleges. However, even at these colleges with relatively low student-faculty ratios, and perhaps a serious concern for the individual student, more than a quarter of the respondents expressed dissatisfaction with the opportunity for social contacts with faculty.

The purpose of this part of the study was to assess respondents' reactions to college facilities and services to determine if dissatisfaction with some of the items contributed to withdrawal. There can be little doubt that dissatisfaction with facilities and services of the colleges contributed to withdrawal in some cases, as evidenced by percentages presented in the following two sections in Table 14, Reasons for Transfer, and in Table 15, Reasons for Discontinuance. Items on those tables which might reflect the expressed dissatisfaction with certain aspects of facilities and services are, "I was generally dissatisfied," "I found the student body different than I expected," and "I was lonesome and unhappy."

Iffert's investigations led him to the conclusion that the percentages of students rating college facilities and services unsatisfactory were lower among dropouts than among those who remained to complete their education. He suggests that withdrawal is more closely related to the inability to endure dissatisfactions than simply to the presence of irritating elements.[29] However, the fact that the percentage of students showing dissatisfaction increases with length of attendance at institutions of higher education does not negate the thesis that dissatisfaction with college facilities and services contributed to the withdrawal of some students. Therefore, college administrators might well review policies and procedures in those areas with a high percentage of unsatisfactory responses if they plan to increase the rate of retention.

[28] *Ibid.*, p. 51.
[29] *Ibid.*

THE TRANSFER STUDENT

Of the 1,102 students who voluntarily withdrew from the twenty-one colleges during the period under study, 777 indicated they had transferred to another institution. A section of the questionnaire was designed specifically to determine the types of institutions to which they transferred and the degree of importance they assigned to various reasons for transfer. The data collected in this section of the questionnaire were augmented by another section inquiring into all students' plans regarding further college attendance as perceived at the time of withdrawal and at the time the questionnaire was completed.

Only 3.5 per cent of the respondents indicated that at the time of withdrawal they had no plans to return to college. At the time the questionnaire was completed, for some as much as two years after withdrawal or transfer, the percentage of respondents not planning to return to college had increased to only 4.3 per cent. The percentage of students who at the time of withdrawal planned to resume college work was 72.3; this proportion had decreased to 63.7 per cent by the time the questionnaire was completed. Eight and three-tenths per cent of the respondents were undecided about future college plans at the time of withdrawal and this percentage had reduced only slightly, to 7.5 per cent, two years later.

It should be recalled that about 75 per cent of the respondents in the study were freshmen and sophomores when they left the colleges studied. Since leaving college about 20 per cent of the respondents had been employed part time and 30 per cent had worked full time. Twenty-two per cent had married. Of the total group of students responding, all of whom withdrew voluntarily, about 30 per cent dropped out of full-time college attendance and approximately 70 per cent transferred to other colleges.

Of the students responding to the transfer section of the questionnaire, 90.7 per cent transferred to larger institutions. Similarly, Iffert found that a high percentage (76.2 per cent) of students transferring from liberal arts colleges entered larger institutions, but he also determined that 71.8 per cent of those who transferred from universities went to smaller institutions.[30] Publicly supported colleges received nearly 62 per cent of the transferring students while church-related institutions received a little more than 13 per cent. It is interesting that Iffert determined that students who originally registered in church-related institutions and later transferred showed the greatest tendency to change to another type of institution. Eighty-nine per cent of the transfer students from non-Catholic church-related institutions followed this pattern.[31]

[30] *Ibid.*, p. 83.
[31] *Ibid.*, p. 85.

TABLE 14. STUDENTS' RATING OF REASONS FOR TRANSFER

Reasons for transfer	Percentages of students judging item of some importance
1. I was generally dissatisfied.	62.08
2. My curriculum interests changed.	47.21
3. I wished to attend a less expensive institution.	44.77
4. I wanted to be in a larger institution.	42.65
5. I wanted a new program that was not offered.	41.82
6. I wanted to be nearer my home town.	30.37
7. I was not interested in what I was studying.	27.30
8. I wanted to attend a more prestigious institution.	23.22
9. My grades were too low to continue.	11.62
10. I wanted to be farther away from home.	9.56
11. I wanted to be in a smaller institution.	2.84

Respondents' reasons for transferring to another institution are reported in descending order of importance in Table 14. The percentages are based on the number of respondents who considered the item of some importance in their decisions to transfer. The degree of importance represented by the percentages ranges from "slight" to "great." Because respondents may have assigned some degree of importance to more than one item, percentages total far more than 100.

The most important reason for transfer, as indicated by student ratings, was "general dissatisfaction." Iffert also received this response and concluded that students transferring from privately controlled institutions independent of church show the greatest discontent, while those transferring from church-related colleges show the least.[32] Student comments give the best insights into the wide variety of reasons for the dissatisfaction experienced by students at these colleges. The dissatisfaction does not always begin with, or result from, the college and sometimes can be traced to the home or the high school. Some representative comments follow:

. . . My biggest problem at college was not knowing what I wanted to do. I had a B average and my father was dissatisfied. Everybody was pushing me to do something different.

I had never wished to go to ——— College, but my parents wanted me to go to a small coed Christian college. . . . The small college town and campus were too restricted in types and backgrounds of people and the fine arts were lacking.

My reasons for transferring really have very little to do with the college in particular. I felt stifled; I had too much energy and too little

[32] Ibid., pp. 85, 87.

freedom. After attending a much larger institution I found that I must either be a number on a large campus or live in a fish bowl on a small campus. Just can't win. [The young lady returned to the original college] . . . primarily because the education there is far superior to that from [larger college]. I figure if you can't have what you want, you might as well get what you should.

The second most frequent cause for transfer was a change in curriculum interest, which was also rated second in the Iffert study.[33] The fifth rated reason, "I wanted a new program that was not offered," is also related to change in curriculum interest. Students enrolled in the Three-Two programs of preprofessional preparation apparently used this option to indicate their reason for transfer, and this was taken into account in analyzing the responses. Iffert attributed the highest percentage of third-year transfers to the Three-Two Plans of liberal arts colleges.[34] Over half of the twenty-one colleges participating in the study have programs of this type.

Curriculum and program reasons for transfer are again best revealed by student comments:

> My main reason for transfer was to bring about a change in curriculum. I was dissatisfied also with many aspects of a small college, but I shall never regret my experience at ——— College. I must admit a whole new world has opened up attending a larger university. It helped in developing my personality and in broadening my interests.

> I was accepted in dental school with the college background I had completed. I had wanted to go to medical school but my grades were lower than most who are accepted into medical school, so I decided to withdraw and go to dental school.

Ranking third on the list of reasons for transfer was a desire to attend a less expensive institution and the fourth was a desire to transfer to a larger one. It was evident that "larger institution" was synonymous with an urban setting. ". . . No decent cultural opportunities—the library, theater, museums, etc., were poor. I wanted a city college in a more liberal and intelligent atmosphere." Another boy said, "I desired the cosmopolitan atmosphere of a large urban university and a school I could be proud of and excited about."

The sixth most frequently cited reason reflected the student's desire to be nearer his home town. Iffert found this item to be chosen more often by students from liberal arts colleges than by students from all other types. It ranked third on his list of students' reasons for transferring from colleges.

[33] *Ibid.,* p. 88.
[34] *Ibid.,* p. 83.

Lack of interest in studies, the seventh most important reason for transfer, is exemplified by the girl who stated, "I believe my reason for leaving college is primarily the fact that learning is an abstract process without any immediate, tangible results. I needed something that would give me those tangible results." A boy said, "I disliked my schedule time-wise and loathed the physical education program. Certain courses were extremely boring."

A desire to attend a more prestigious institution was rated eighth on the list and was usually coupled with other dissatisfactions, as in the case of the boy who wrote, "I desired more personal and social liberty and I wanted to attend a school with a bigger name, both in athletics and academics."

Transfer because of low grades ranked ninth on the list and held little significance. However, this item is of interest in that one student described a situation that is probably repeated often where college officials ask a student to withdraw for a term or longer. This student said, "I was requested to stay out of school a term and decided to stay out longer. . . ." He went on to say, "I feel I have been unfairly evaluated in several classes causing this academic probation." He was nevertheless listed on college records as a voluntary withdrawal.

The final reasons, wishing to live farther from home and wanting to attend a smaller institution, ranked tenth and eleventh, but the response was insignificant and there were no comments giving additional information on these reasons.

Comments revealed that a great number of students planned to transfer at the time they were admitted. Their reasons vary from financial to bargaining with parents, as these examples illustrate:

> I attended ——— College to save some money by commuting and paying lower tuition to finish three years, and then I graduated from the University of ——— which was my first choice.

> I planned to transfer long before entering ——— College, because I wanted to study pharmacy. I went to ——— College first because I had friends there and I felt I might adjust easier by attending a small college first.

> I knew when I entered that I would only be at ——— College for a year as my father wanted me to go to the school he taught at, and we compromised.

Thus, general dissatisfaction ranked first as a reason for transfer and was followed by changing curriculum interests, the desire to attend a less expensive institution, and the desire to pursue programs not offered by the institution in which the student was enrolled. Other items show lesser but still important degrees of influence on the students' deci-

TABLE 15.   REASONS FOR DISCONTINUANCE RATED OF
MODERATE OR GREAT IMPORTANCE

Reasons	Percentages of 1102 respondents		
	MEN	WOMEN	TOTAL
Financial (self)	29.91	17.41	22.69
Financial (family)	22.65	19.78	20.96
I lacked interest in my studies	26.07	16.14	20.33
I found the student body different than I expected	12.39	18.35	15.79
I was lonesome and unhappy	13.25	17.09	15.43
I planned to be married soon	5.77	20.73	14.43
I was discouraged by low grades	15.39	7.12	10.71
I took a full-time job	8.98	6.96	7.81
Illness or physical disability (self)	7.27	7.81	7.63
My housing situation caused trouble	5.98	6.96	6.54
Placed on probation for academic reasons	10.26	2.01	6.08
I was needed at home	5.77	5.06	5.26
Illness or physical disability (family)	3.85	5.70	4.99
I found college work too difficult	6.19	3.16	4.45
Commuting took too long	2.99	2.06	2.45
Military service (enlisted)	3.64	0.16	1.63
I had marital difficulties	1.92	0.63	1.18
Placed on probation for reasons other than academic	1.28	0.79	1.09
I wanted to participate more fully in the civil rights movement	0.86	0.79	0.81
Military service (drafted)	1.49	0.16	0.72

sions to transfer. It is clear that no one reason for transfer or withdrawal ever exists. The student comments reported in this part of the
study witness strongly to the "multicausality" of transfer described by
Summerskill and others.[35]

STUDENTS' REASONS FOR DISCONTINUANCE

In that portion of the questionnaire dealing with reasons for discontinuing college, options were purposely limited to those reflecting
on the student rather than on the institution which he left. Table 15
shows the percentage of 1,102 students rating each item to be "of
moderate or great importance" in their decisions to discontinue their college careers. Items are arranged in descending order of importance
based on percentages in the total column. Percentages again total more
than 100, because some students may have chosen more than one option.

[35] Summerskill, *op. cit.*, p. 649.

An examination of Table 15 reveals that financial considerations ranked first among reasons for discontinuing college work, followed by a lack of interest in study. Next in order of importance were two items which deal with failure to make friends or to adjust to the social features of college life—"I was lonesome and unhappy," and "I found the student body different than I expected." Another item which received a significant number of responses was, "I planned to be married soon." Iffert's data, when adjusted to eliminate the high percentages concerned with military reasons due to the Korean War, reflect basically the same ratings obtained in this study.

It must be kept in mind in any analysis of the total percentages presented in Table 15 that respondents were skewed toward women by a ratio of 57 to 43. However, it appears that the ranking order of those percentages in the total column would remain about the same if the respondents were evenly divided between men and women. Nevertheless, a marked difference between male and female rating patterns does exist and it may be instructive to examine this difference.

Men generally withdrew from these twenty-one colleges for financial and for academic reasons. Financial reasons were also the cause of a substantial number of female withdrawals, but academic reasons played a weaker role than was the case with men. Marriage and social reasons for discontinuance—"I planned to be married soon," and "I found the student body different than I expected"—were important for women. The difference in rating patterns may be related to the fact that, generally speaking, women do not attend college for exactly the same reasons as do men. If expectations are different, it follows that reasons for discontinuance would also vary.

Over 15 per cent of the students took the opportunity to write other reasons for discontinuing college, but most such comments referred to personal problems rather than to college facilities or services.

Summary

In an effort to determine why students at twenty-one liberal arts colleges left their college of first enrollment, the present study has concentrated on voluntary withdrawals in these colleges. This emphasis was chosen because in twenty of the twenty-one institutions students who withdrew of their own volition outnumbered those who withdrew involuntarily by more than two to one. Knowledge of the backgrounds, reasons for attending college, reactions to certain aspects of college life, and reasons for withdrawal provided by these students may enable the colleges in question to devise programs aimed at reducing the attrition rate.

Results of the study indicate that students rated occupational reasons for going to college first, followed by academic, traditional, personal-self, and social service reasons. Both men and women ranked occupational reasons for attending college first, but women gave greater weight than men to the influence of academic, personal-self, and social service reasons.

Although, in almost every case, a majority of students rated statements dealing with college facilities and services "satisfactory," more than half of the items were rated "unsatisfactory" by 25 per cent or more of the respondents. Statements concerned with counseling, guidance, and orientation services were accorded the greatest percentages of "unsatisfactory" responses, as were those statements dealing with the availability of on- and off-campus recreational facilities. It is not unexpected that students who withdrew from these colleges should find fault with certain of the facilities and services offered. Moreover, counseling services would be a reasonable choice for expressed dissatisfaction because the students in question would have convinced themselves that they received poor or insufficient advice when they sought it. But the strong possibility remains that the students may be justified in their negative reactions to these services. Consequently, an improvement in the counseling, guidance, and orientation services at these institutions may result in a lower attrition rate.

Seventy per cent of the respondents transferred to other institutions. Ratings of reasons for transfer ranked general dissatisfaction first, followed by a change in curriculum interests; expense of education ranked third, while low grades were rated of some importance by about 12 per cent of the students responding. It was also evident in many student comments that a large number of entering students did not plan to remain for four years.

Financial reasons for leaving college, concerned with either the student or his family, ranked highest for both men and women. The relatively high ranking of the item, "I wished to attend a less expensive institution," among reasons for transfer also sounds this theme. Men and women differed somewhat in their ratings of other reasons for discontinuance. Marriage was the single reason rated highest by women, followed by dissatisfaction with the student body, and loneliness. Men were more affected by academically related reasons.

In these institutions a smaller percentage of the women than of the men withdrew involuntarily. This fact, when coupled with the comparatively lower ratings given to items concerned with academic problems as reasons for discontinuance by women, may reflect the more stringent academic admission requirements for women in institutions of higher education. Thus, increasing the academic requirements for admission appears to be a simple way to reduce attrition, but one which may not be favored because of conflicting fiscal or academic policy.

Seventeen of the colleges supplied information in response to a request for reports of institutional studies, programs, and other activities carried out to affect attrition. The studies in which these institutions were involved ranged from simple statistical summaries to comprehensive long-range follow-up studies.

A review of these programs designed to study or affect attrition revealed wide differences among institutions, with statistical studies of census data being most common. Only six colleges indicate an established framework for collecting these data yearly and reporting them in a standardized manner. Seven colleges indicated they made contact through questionnaires with students who withdrew. Although few of the institutions presently have continuing programs, some plan to carry out this type of research in the future. They described a wide variety of counseling and curricular programs designed to cope with student disinterest in studies and to assist with academic problems. These programs tend to concentrate on the freshman year.

As this material was prepared, a number of questions needing further analysis were discovered. Why, for example, do students transfer from church-related colleges to non-church-related institutions? Why is withdrawal a profitable learning experience for some while others are lost and become dropouts, and what obligation does the college have to ensure the former? How do students choose the college they will attend? What can be done to improve the experiences students find unsatisfactory without adversely affecting those already highly satisfactory? Is finance a real problem for students? The list of urgent questions grows with reflection.

This analysis can serve to familiarize administrators with those experiences considered important by students who have voluntarily withdrawn. No such study, however, can reduce the need for individual institutions to study their own possible causes of attrition and disseminate the findings to all members of the college staff.

BIOGRAPHIES

LANDRUM R. BOLLING, a former war correspondent, free-lance writer, and Professor of Political Science, currently serves as President of Earlham College. Born in Tennessee, Dr. Bolling received his B.A. from the University of Tennessee and his M.A. from the University of Chicago. He is co-author of *This Is Germany* and author of *City Manager Government in Dayton.*

DANA L. FARNSWORTH is Director of the Harvard University Health Services and Henry K. Oliver Professor of Hygiene at Harvard. Formerly he served as Medical Director, Massachusetts Institute of Technology. Among his writings are *Mental Health in College and University* and (with Fred V. Hine) *Living.* A native of West Virginia, he received his A.B. and B.S. from West Virginia University and his M.D. from Harvard.

DAVID E. FOX received his B.S. from the State University College at Geneseo, New York, and his M.A. from Teachers College, Columbia University. He is presently serving as Assistant to the President, State University College at Geneseo.

JB LON HEFFERLIN, a native of Montana, is Associate Director of the Institute of Higher Education's Study of Institutional Vitality. He received his A.B. from Harvard and his M.A. and Ph.D. from Stanford University. Dr. Hefferlin's publications include several articles, reports, and reviews relating to higher education.

EARL J. MCGRATH, a long-time student of higher education, has held virtually every position in the field of educational administration. Formerly United States Commissioner of Education and President of the University

121

of Kansas City, he now serves as Director of the Institute of Higher Education and Chairman of the Department of Higher Education, Teachers College, Columbia University, and is Chancellor of Eisenhower College. Dr. McGrath is author, co-author, or editor of many works on higher education, including *Memo to a College Faculty Member, Are Liberal Arts Colleges Becoming Professional Schools?,* and *The Quantity and Quality of College Teachers.*

C. ROBERT PACE is a native of Minnesota and received his B.A. from De-Pauw University and his M.A. and Ph.D. from the University of Minnesota. A psychologist who has held teaching and administrative posts in higher education, he is currently Professor of Higher Education, University of California at Los Angeles. His writings include *They Went to College, Evaluation in Teacher Education,* and the *College and University Environment Scales.*

NEVITT SANFORD is Director of the Institute for the Study of Human Problems, Stanford University. A native of Virginia, he is well known as a psychologist and educator. He has served as a research psychologist at Harvard, as Professor of Psychology at the University of California at Berkeley, and as Coordinator, Mary Conover Mellon Foundation. Dr. Sanford has been author, co-author, or editor of many books, including *Physique, Personality and Scholarship, The Authoritarian Personality,* and *The American College.* He received his A.B. from the University of Richmond, his M.A. from Columbia, and his Ph.D. from Harvard.

ROBERT J. SOLOMON is Vice-President and Director of General Testing Services Programs, Educational Testing Service. A native of New York City, he received his B.S. and M.A. from New York University and has contributed to many publications in the field of social studies.

W. MAX WISE, whose writings include *They Came for the Best of Reasons —College Students Today,* is Director, Graduate Fellowship Program, Danforth Foundation. Dr. Wise received his B.A. from the State University of Iowa and his M.A. and Ed.D. from Teachers College, Columbia University. He formerly served as a secondary school teacher in Iowa, as Dean of Student Personnel at the University of Florida, and as Professor of Education at Teachers College.

378.1981
M14   **Date Due**   91794

Reserve				
1 3 71				
Bro Paul Gross				
AUG 1 9 1971				